A PASSIONATE COMMITMENT

RECAPTURING YOUR SENSE OF PURPOSE

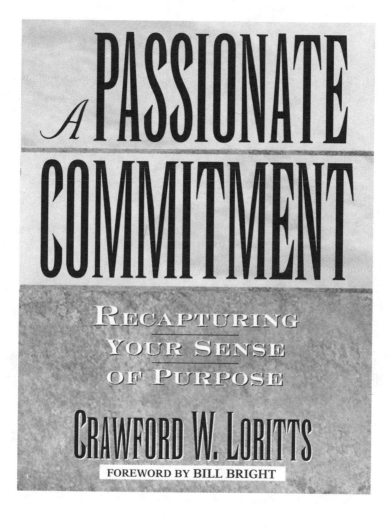

A PASSIONATE COMMITMENT

RECAPTURING YOUR SENSE OF PURPOSE

CRAWFORD W. LORITTS

FOREWORD BY BILL BRIGHT

MOODY PRESS
CHICAGO

ISBN: 0-8024-5246-9

5 7 9 10 8 6 4

Printed in the United States of America

This book is dedicated to my partner
in life and ministry—my wife, Karen.
She models a passionate commitment to
Christ and she is the wind beneath my wings.

CONTENTS

FOREWORD

ince 1951 Campus Crusade for Christ has been committed to encouraging Christians to live lives of faith and purpose. Through large training conferences, outreach events, one-to-one discipleship, and distribution of our materials, we have sought to mobilize Christians to help fulfill the Great Commission in obedience to our Lord.

That is why I consider it a special privilege to write the foreword to this very important book by my beloved friend and co-laborer, Crawford Loritts.

A Passionate Commitment comes at a critical point in the history of the church. Apathy and materialism have dulled the impact of our message. We need a clear, challenging call to return to the essence of New Testament Christianity and to the exciting, abundant life our Savior offers each of His obedient children. This is God's purpose for our lives.

The principles discussed in this book will not only help you recapture your sense of purpose, but they also will help you maintain that purpose. This is a book that demands to be read more than once—and shared with others.

Crawford Loritts's life and ministry visibly illustrate what he writes about. God has honored Crawford's own *passionate commitment.* He is one of the most effective leaders and communicators I know. He is also one of the most popular among our staff of more than 15,000 serving our Lord in approximately 150 countries. I have heard Crawford speak to large crowds, have interacted with him in meetings, and have spent personal time with him in prayer and fellowship. His ministry is an extension of his walk with God.

As you read this book, I trust you will be as blessed and challenged to follow our Lord as I have been.

Bill Bright,
President and Founder
Campus Crusade for Christ International

ACKNOWLEDGMENTS

riting a book is more than a notion—it's hard work. This revised edition of *A Passionate Commitment* is the product of the encouragement of some wonderful people . . .

Greg Thornton, vice president of Moody Press, read the original book and had the vision for a revised edition with a study guide. Thanks, Greg, not only for your partnership in this project but also for your friendship and fellowship in the Cause.

Jim Bell and Cheryl Dunlop of the editing team at Moody Press have made an invaluable contribution. Thanks, Cheryl and Jim, for your creativity and helping me to put this edition in a readable condition.

The friendship and helpful suggestions of John Perkins have meant a lot to me. Thanks, John, for your thoughtful response to the manuscript.

Leonard Scott, my executive assistant, helps to keep me going in the right direction. Thanks, Scottie, for helping to rearrange my priorities to meet deadlines.

A special thanks to our Legacy staff team. Their commitment to the Savior and to His call for our ministry both humbles me and gives me a "flesh and blood" picture of what *a passionate commitment* looks like.

My parents, Crawford and Sylvia Loritts, pointed me to Calvary. On July 4, 1995, my father went home to be with the Lord. Pop taught me to hang in there and not walk away from responsibility. Maybe one day soon I'll write a book about some of the other lessons he taught me.

Karen and our four children are the greatest team in the world. Thank you for your model of commitment and encouragement. Your support has made ministry a joy.

1

GETTING THE MOST OUT OF LIFE

Monuments to Materialism vs. Prominence of Christ

Darryl Hicks is thirty-five years old. He is respected as a loving husband and father, a faithful church member, and a successful and honest attorney.

At sixteen he invited Christ into his life and began to grow immediately. He developed a consistent spiritual discipline, spending an hour each morning in Bible study and prayer. He started praying fervently for his family and his non-Christian friends. He consistently made time to go out with the church youth group every Thursday evening to share Christ with others.

Even in college, despite the demands of his challenging courses and a heavy work schedule, he made time for his personal spiritual nurture and ministry opportunities. He attended the weekly meetings of one of the Christian groups on his campus and went with them to several conferences throughout the year. He dropped out of college for a year after his mother died and he found himself needing time to research and pray about some questions he had, but he returned with his faith stronger than ever.

The guy was incredible. He even found time for a social life, and he and Margaret Bailey began dating occasionally in their sophomore year. By the end of their junior year things got serious between them. They became engaged and two weeks after graduation they were married.

Throughout law school Darryl continued his service for Christ. He and Margaret joined a local church in their community and became very active. Darryl served as youth adviser and chairman of the outreach committee.

Things were "working" for Darryl and Margaret. During Darryl's time at law school Margaret gave birth to the first of their three children, a boy. Financially, things were tight, but as a couple they were very happy.

Darryl graduated from law school with honors, passed the bar examination the first time around, and was recruited by a prestigious law firm. Because of his brilliance and diligence, Darryl became successful in a relatively short time. In fact, after only four years with the firm he was asked to become a partner. Finally, the years of sacrifice and hard work were paying off, and in a big way.

The success, in a strange way, was bittersweet. It is true they were well off financially—they bought a beautiful, spacious home; they owned two late model cars; they even bought a condominium in the mountains. But Darryl often would be in the office by seven in the morning, and he seldom left before seven or eight in the evening, including some Saturdays. With three children, the endless pressures of his law practice, his civic commitment, and the growing need to spend quality time with Margaret, Darryl began to feel squeezed. He felt it particularly strongly in his spiritual life. In the past he had known a refreshing sense of joy and an endless supply of spiritual energy. Now, where there was once a burning desire to obey God and minister to the needs of others, he experienced dryness. His was a cold, mechanical Christianity.

One evening, Darryl and Margaret invited their best friends, a couple from their church, over for dinner. As their time together drew to a close, Darryl told of his spiritual struggle. "I am not experiencing the same passionate commitment to Christ that I once had. Although I still read my Bible and pray," he said, "I have lost my sense of mission and purpose as a Christian."

One friend asked, "Why do you think that has happened?"

"I don't know; I guess I'm just consumed by all the demands of the present."

As their friends were leaving, Darryl commented, "Although I'm thankful for my success, I know there is much more to life. I know God wants much more from me."

SPIRITUAL APATHY

I wish I could say Darryl's struggle is unique. It is not. He suffers from the same spiritual paralysis that grips much of contemporary Christianity. Many wonderful people outwardly have a fine Christian life. They go to church every Sunday, perhaps even attend prayer meetings, give their money to the church and other Christian ministries, have nice families, read their Bibles, and pray. Yet, underneath all the Christian activity there is a coldness and, at times, a confusion about the place and prominence of Jesus Christ in their inner lives.

It is a painfully sad and all too familiar reality that the pressures of life and the apathetic materialism in our society have caused the world to be more "salt and light" to us than we have been to the world. I deeply believe that these are the most threatening times in terms of impact for the cause of Christ that have been known in the history of the church. Admittedly, that is a strong statement. Take a look around you, though. Even as I write these words several of our prominent Christian leaders have had to leave the ministry in disgrace. Others have preached a gospel of self-indulgence and personal prosperity, and they have led thousands down this trail of perverted Christianity. No wonder some of their "ministries" have been plagued with financial impropriety, donor scams, and a legacy of monuments to materialism, to say nothing of the moral offenses—all done in the name of the Lord!

What about the crucified life?

What about being conformed to the sufferings of Christ? No, you can't have your cake and eat it too. That spells worldliness in the truest sense. We may be on our way to becoming the apathetic students of Satan's discipleship program.

And that's the point.

The self-centered apathy of our culture has produced a compromised Christianity, which has in turn produced a directionless Christianity—a Christianity that only responds, but does not initiate.

As we look at Darryl, and as we examine our own lives, we see clearly how compromise (which is usually subtle) will eventually produce fruitlessness. Darryl represents a Christianity that is in the vicinity, but not really at the right location.

CHRISTIAN ASSUMPTIONS

A few years ago my wife, Karen, and I were invited to a friend's house for dinner. We had been to their home before and I was familiar with the area, so I thought there would be no problem finding the house. Wrong! We drove around for more than an hour, frustrated because we knew we were only a few blocks away, but we couldn't find the place. Not only were we lost, but I also had to deal with Karen's I-told-you-so's. This experience is a reminder that assumptions can get a person into trouble. A quick phone call before we left the house would have saved us from all that hassle and stress.

Assumptions have gotten many Christians into spiritual hot water. Jesus Christ came to give us an abundant, fruitful Christianity, filled with specific direction and purpose. Although we have a general sense of direction, many of us have assumed either that somehow we can work out the details or that everything will fall into place. We fail to realize that we do not live in a favorable or even a neutral environment. Every day our commitment to Christ is assaulted by the world, the flesh, or the devil. Therefore, our Christianity must take the *offensive*–it must be *intentional.*

I am convinced that many of us have a general sense of purpose, but, in terms of the internal direction of our lives and the peace that comes from submitting our wills to God's, we're confused. We suffer from the same problem Darryl has. We outwardly conform to what we say we believe, but inwardly there is coldness. We privately confess that we know God wants and deserves more from us.

The critical question is: How do we recapture our sense of purpose? That's what this book is about. I am a fellow pilgrim with you in the struggle to maintain my sense of mission and direction in the Christian life. I want to assure you that God, through the power of the Holy Spirit, will help us to see clearly the direction in which we need to go. He will reveal to us the critical ingredients needed to recover a sense of freshness in our Christian lives and, thus, a sense of mission.

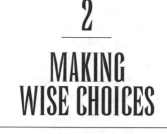

2
MAKING
WISE CHOICES

Solomon's Five Crucial Principles

 here's a lot of truth in that old saying, "The only thing
we learn from history is that we don't learn anything
at all from history."

I'm a child of the post-World War II baby boom. We've
heard an awful lot about the baby boomers in recent years, both
good and bad. My generation has shaped the values of American
society as none other in the twentieth century. We have experienced a lot.

In fact, I've identified a four-phase shift in emphasis on values, spanning the past forty years, to which all the baby boomers
have had a front row seat. From 1946 to 1960, America labored
under a philosophy of personal peace and materialism. In other
words, we just didn't want any more bad news. We had crawled
out of the Great Depression; we'd been through a horrible war;
now we were eager to let the good times roll. We craved prosperity. We wanted our slice of the economic pie—a single family
home, a couple of cars in the garage, and maybe even a little
vacation cottage on the lake.

Some of our parents overcompensated for the hard times
they had experienced. For example, my parents frequently
reminded my two sisters and me that they didn't want us to have
it as hard as they did during the Depression. So they provided
for more than our wants and cushioned us from some of the
hard knocks. No, we were not well off. Dad was simply determined to do the very best he could for his family, partially, I'm

convinced, because he was haunted by the economic horrors of his Depression generation. He would remind us of how he had to walk several miles to school and of the times when all they had to eat was beans. I can understand his wanting us to have it better. As I look back, though, I think a little sacrifice and a bit of suffering for us baby boomers could have made us a little less selfish and might have strengthened our character.

Enter the next phase. Between 1960 and 1968, education was the order of the day. That's not to say that we abandoned the pursuit of materialism; there just was a heightened emphasis on higher education during this period. So off we went to flood the hallowed halls of higher learning. We thought that if we could study the great minds and master the great academic disciplines, we could unlock the door to significance and success in life. We also would be able to solve all the problems of the world.

In 1968, though, the pleasant dream was interrupted by a nightmare. We were officially into the third phase: drugs and revolution.

Nineteen sixty-eight was some year! It brought the escalation of the war in Vietnam; the assassinations of Bobby Kennedy and Martin Luther King, Jr.; and the emergence of a drug-pushing prophet named Timothy Leary, a former Harvard professor turned grand pied piper of the drug culture.

Our hopes were shattered. The youth culture felt powerless. Our heroes were gone. Our friends and loved ones were being blown up in a war that, apparently, we were not committed to winning. Trust in our government was rapidly deteriorating. We demanded change. We responded with anger and activism. We marched, picketed, sat in, and even burned a few cities. Some of us fled the country. Others succumbed to Leary's gospel of LSD, choosing to drop out completely. LSD gave my generation a "mind-expanding" magic carpet ride. We thought that drugs could solve the problems of the individual and that revolution could solve the collective problems of society. It has been a long journey. In fact, some still have not returned from the trip.

However, in 1972 we began to enter the fourth phase, which we are still in. We reverted to phase one, personal peace and materialism, but with a strong, malignant dose of *apathy.*

In the early seventies things began to settle down. In 1972 President Nixon put the brakes on the Vietnam War. Leary's followers realized that their minds were being exploded rather than expanded through LSD. Many of the activists traded their pickets for three-piece, pin-striped suits and seats in the board room, city hall, and Congress.

TODAY'S PRIORITIES

Now, I suspect the pendulum has swung too far. I applaud the progress we are making; and I certainly am not in favor of violence, drugs, or anarchy. However, I must admit I find the apathetic materialism more frightening than the revolutionary atmosphere of 1969. At that time, Christianity had a clear context. You knew where you stood, and you knew where biblical Christianity stood—in stark contrast to the lifestyle of the time. Today it's not so clear.

At least in the 1960s we seemed to be concerned about others (even if we only gave lip service to that concern). Not so today. I get the distinct impression that the only cause many of us are committed to is our cause. It's *my* agenda. What's in it for me?

Even some (not all) of the Christian "activism" leaves me flat. I can't help but question the motives of some of my brothers and sisters who recently have discovered the political process. Don't get me wrong; all citizens, including responsible Christians, have an obligation to be involved in the political process. I wonder sometimes, though, are we involved because we want to see societal change for the good of the individual, or are we involved because we want to be in power and control? While some may want merely to protect individual rights, the compassionate Christian will be driven to be used of God as an expression of His love and forgiveness in the world in which we live.

The apathetic materialism of our society has had much more influence on us than we'd like to admit. The pressure of living in this era is one of the most powerful reasons many Christians have become cold and indifferent. We have redesigned our theology in order to make it more palatable. We now have a cul-

tural Christianity that allows us to acquire as much as we want
with little self-sacrifice and virtually no eternal values.

WISE AND FOOLISH CHOICES

King Solomon was one of the wealthiest and wisest men of
all times. In today's dollars, one scholar said, he would not be
simply a multi-millionaire, but a multi-_billion_aire. I guess you
could say almost everything he touched turned to gold.

Solomon wrote three books of the Bible: Proverbs (most of
it), the Song of Solomon, and Ecclesiastes. In Ecclesiastes,
Solomon opens his heart and reveals his deepest feelings and his
philosophy of life. It's almost as if he were leaving a legacy for
succeeding generations. It is interesting to note what Solomon
does _not_ say in this book.

He does not give us a formula for material success.

He does not tell us how to become prominent and affluent.

Solomon goes deeper than that; he talks about what he has
learned through his successes and failures in life.

I believe that the book of Ecclesiastes has a prophetic message for our time and society. It brings us face to face with some
key principles through which we can restructure our value system. Considering these principles will help us think biblically
about our lifestyle and the purpose of life.

The overriding message of Ecclesiastes, simply stated, is: _It
is foolish and destructive to think that the center of life is material gain._

Solomon tells us we should enjoy life and the comforts that
may come our way; however, he reminds us repeatedly that "all
is vanity"—empty and fleeting.

FIVE CRUCIAL PRINCIPLES

Solomon supports his proposition by giving us five crucial
principles, lessons from an enormously successful man (at least
in the eyes of the world). These principles are not necessarily
sequential, but are interwoven throughout the book. So, rather
than giving the specific passages, let me encourage you to take
note of the principles and read the book for yourself.

The Emptiness of Human Wisdom

The first principle is:

In the ultimate sense, human wisdom is empty.

It is important that we look at what Solomon does *not* mean. He is not saying we should not have educational or intellectual goals. He is not saying we should not use our God-given mental faculties to solve our problems or to plan and set goals for the future.

He *is* saying that no matter how brilliant we are, human minds are limited. Our wisdom is empty in that it cannot direct or control our destiny. The human mind, the intricate, marvelous wonder that it is, is not greater than God. Even our "collective" mind can never replace God or solve the problems that we face as human beings: greed, poverty, war, injustice, etc.

That's why humanism is such a futile philosophy. For humanism contends that man, not God, is the center of the universe and that through our systematic, purposeful, intellectual development we (mankind) will be able to eradicate our problems and usher in utopia.

The reality of the human predicament glaringly contradicts what humanists believe. Despite our technology and despite the wonderful advances we've made in medicine, science, the arts, and engineering, a strong case can be made that society is not getting better—it's getting worse. The lack of morality, the degree of greed and injustice is intensifying. Yes, sin has become more "sophisticated"; but, in the name of intellectual and moral honesty, we are forced to declare that we are nowhere close to utopia.

Solomon's words must stand as a solemn warning. Yes, develop your mind. Use your ability to think; apply wisdom to life's choices—but always remember that only God can control our future, and only God can correct the evil that is in society.

Unchangeable Laws

Solomon says that human wisdom cannot stand alone; it is empty. Nor can human wisdom replace God—it must *depend upon* God.

The *second principle* is:

We must all face the laws which govern life.

Despite Solomon's privileged position as the son of David, who was the greatest king Israel ever had, he realized that his wealth and wisdom did not exempt him from the pain and pressures of life.

None of us, in fact, is exempt. It is painful for us to admit: but if we live long enough, we will all experience deep disappointment. That's why it is so important to distance our sense of self-worth and significance from our aspirations in life. By all means we should have dreams; but we need to realize that worth as human beings is not tied to what we do—it is tied to who we are; creatures created in the image of God.

Not long ago I spoke in a chapel service for a prominent NFL team. As I looked at those athletes, many of whose names are household words, I was aware that in a few short hours these men would be playing a game that represented everything they had dreamed of since high school days.

I said to them, "Pretty soon you will take the short bus ride from the hotel to the stadium. You will tape up and put your uniform on; you'll go over the game plan one more time; then you will run out of the tunnel onto the playing field where you'll be greeted by seventy thousand cheering fans. Adrenaline will rush through your body. You'll be 'pumped' because you will be living out your lifelong ambition, and you will be rewarded with more money in one season than most of the people in the world will make in a lifetime.

"You've succeeded and it's sweet. Congratulations.

"But in one split second it could all end—a twisted knee, a helmet in your spinal column—and just that quickly the ride is over. What happens next? Where is your self-esteem?"

Temporary Treasures

There are drastic, shattering disappointments in life. We must look to God for our hope and significance so that when our dreams are not realized, our plans change, or unanticipated suffering comes our way, our personal sense of meaning and worth is not destroyed.

That leads to the *third principle:*

There is no lasting value in earthly goods and treasures.

Remember, this comes from a man who had it all.

Unfortunately, in our society a person's significance is determined by the "things" that he has: the kind of house he lives in, the car he drives, the clothes he wears, and even the kind of people he is seen with (people, too, can be treated as things). If you have a lot of the right "things," you win.

Ironically, that which we think brings the greatest satisfaction often is the cause of our dissatisfaction. No, I am not saying that we should not have nice houses, cars, clothes, etc. I am saying that things can never be the source of our happiness and joy. Take it from Solomon, who had it all, and probably enjoyed it, but found that nothing he possessed could give him lasting happiness.

The reason materialism is so addictive is that it is based on the wrong assumption: "The more I have, the happier I'll be." When "things" break, get old or wear out, or our mood changes, we're no longer "happy." So *the cure*, we think, *is to get more things*. Enjoy life and the things of life; but God and His purposes must be the source of our true joy and happiness—not fads, fashions, or expectations of others.

Humble Gratitude

As to the *fourth principle*, Solomon says:

We must be humbly grateful for our lot in life.

This principle applies to Solomon's position and success. As an older man now, he has come to appreciate more fully his lofty position as king of Israel, the most powerful kingdom in the then-known world. He realized that much of his prominence was beyond his control. It was not his choice to be born heir to the throne of David—he could have been born one of the enemies of God. Certainly Solomon used his abilities as a wise and skillful leader, but there is no way that all of his fame and fortune could have been the product of personal orchestration. He knew he was blessed indeed.

When you stop to think about it, that's why arrogance and pride are so stupid. None of us selected our parents, and the truth is that our success is more a gift of God than a result of our own personal maneuvers.

Racism is one of the most ridiculous of our social sins. If we didn't select our parents, we certainly didn't choose the color of our skin. A certain race could occupy a position of influence and power in a country for a moment, but that, too, may be temporary. Any one of us could have been born heirs to poverty and oppression. No, we shouldn't pride ourselves in things we have no control over.

Every benefit and every opportunity comes from the hand of a loving, gracious God. Many of us baby boomers have deceived ourselves into thinking that we have made ourselves what we are (whatever that is). I have even detected a strange form of "Christian humanism" which says we did it ourselves— we're in control of our own direction and destiny.

Life After Life

As my late pastor used to say, we must be careful to give God the glory in *everything,* because at any moment God can say, "Give Me back My breath." We certainly need to be humbly grateful for our lot in life.

Finally, the *fifth principle* is:

We must live our lives with the understanding that there is life after death.

The writer of Hebrews points out that in this life we have no continuing city, but we look for a city whose architect and builder is God (Hebrews 11:10).

This world is not our ultimate destination; it's not home. Many Christians live as if the here and now is *it*—we must get all we can, spend all we can, and be as accepted as we can because this life is our only chance.

Sure, God intends us to enjoy life here and now. In fact, in the book of Ecclesiastes you will see that Solomon endorses living life to the hilt—within the parameters of what's right and what's wrong from God's point of view. Enjoy life and have a wonderful time.

That can be done best when we live our lives with the understanding that we are accountable to a holy and just God for the values and choices we adopt along the way. We are citizens of heaven with a temporary residence and work permit in the world. As Christians we live with eternity in our hearts. We interpret life based upon what is eternal, not temporal. We make choices based upon what God wants to do through our lives. We are people who are under the command and direction of Someone else.

The apostle Paul reminds us that all our "works" (our activities, values, motives, etc.) will be tested by fire to see if they are wood, hay, or stubble—the perishable things—or gold, silver, or precious stones—the imperishable (1 Corinthians 3:1–15). Ultimately, only what we do for Christ and His kingdom will last. Those things are the gold, silver, and precious stones.

Since we are creatures of destiny, and because heaven is real to us and we will be held accountable, then it makes all the difference in the world how we live our lives. The choices and decisions we make determine the effectiveness of our lives. If we compromise and give in to our lusts and self-centeredness, we not only hurt ourselves, but we also bring reproach upon the cause of Christ and biblical Christianity. We can't have it both ways. Joy and significance are the products of obedience.

Maintaining our sense of purpose means choosing and affirming the right values. Living life with the understanding that there is life after death means being a follower of Christ, here and now; and that's what we want to look at in the next chapter.

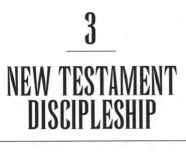

NEW TESTAMENT DISCIPLESHIP

What Discipleship Is Not

ietrich Bonhoeffer says in his classic book, *The Cost of Discipleship,* "The only place to follow Christ is in the world."

At first glance that appears to be a nice, simple saying that captures the obvious, but the more you ponder it, the more profound it becomes. Bonhoeffer is saying the key to effective Christianity is to faithfully follow Christ in the context of the world.

As mentioned earlier, this world does not belong to us; therefore, it is not our ultimate objective. As Christians, our responsibility is not to draw our source of fulfillment and pleasure from the world, but to *influence* the world toward God's purposes and His righteousness. Our posture should not be one of reacting to the standards of the world, but of reflecting the peace, joy, and purpose that comes only through a relationship with Jesus Christ. However, one reason many Christians have lost their sense of purpose is that their perspective on biblical Christianity and its relationship to the values, issues, and structure of this fallen world has become clouded.

Unfortunately, a trend among Christians these days is to retreat and withdraw from the world. We have become confused. Somehow we think our effectiveness as followers of Christ is determined by the number of Bible studies and seminars we attend. We surround ourselves with the Christian community and make sure our children have limited, if any, contact with the non-Christian world. Then we pat ourselves on the back and boast of our faithfulness as "followers of Christ."

Christian activity does not necessarily mean that we are following Christ. Don't misunderstand: Bible study, fellowship with other Christians, and taking part in various Christian activities are essential to our growth. However, they are only a means to an end.

These activities can equip and encourage us to make an impact for Christ and to provide answers and hope for this fallen world. But we cannot influence anything or anyone we do not touch. We must rub shoulders with the world. While guarding against the godless influence of the world, we must be instruments of God's love, and that means getting involved in the lives of non-Christians.

What then does it mean to be a follower of Jesus Christ?

It is to be involved in New Testament discipleship, which is actually a lifelong process and pilgrimage. In fact, the word *disciple* means to be a follower, a learner. Discipleship is not so much a *point* as it is a *process,* an ongoing, continuous process of "living out" what we say we believe. In other words, we will never reach a point in this life where we can claim we have "arrived" or we have been "discipled." (I do think it is legitimate to say we have been "discipled" in the sense that we have come to understand and experience the foundational truths of our relationship with Christ.)

Let's look at two passages from the New Testament which give us the nature and essence of discipleship. The first passage tells us what discipleship should not be, and the second tells us what it should be.

First, what discipleship should not be, seen in Luke 9:57–62:

> As they were going along the road, someone said to Him, "I will follow You wherever You go." And Jesus said to him, "The foxes have holes and the birds of the air have nests, but the Son of Man has nowhere to lay his head." And He said to another, "Follow Me." But he said, "Lord, permit me first to go and bury my father." But He said to him, "Allow the dead to bury their own dead; but as for you, go and proclaim everywhere the king-

dom of God." And another also said, "I will follow You, Lord; but first permit me to say good-bye to those at home." But Jesus said to him, "No one, after putting his hand to the plow and looking back, is fit for the kingdom of God."

In this passage Jesus challenges three people to follow Him. However, their responses show us, in principle, what discipleship is not and should not be. There are some relevant applications to our lives.

THE "VERBALLY COMMITTED DISCIPLE"

The first confrontation we will look at is introduced in verse 57. I call this person the "verbally committed disciple." Jesus and His disciples were going along the crowded road to Jerusalem when apparently this man recognized Jesus the Nazarene. The man approached the Savior and declared, "I will follow You wherever You go."

It is important to note that this exchange took place during the first half of Christ's earthly ministry, while He still rode a crestwave of curiosity, if not popularity. The crowds flocked to Him. Undoubtedly, some were attracted by His miracles and popularity, but others found hope and power in His message.

However, it is clear that the notoriety and possibly the miracles rather than the message drew this "verbally committed disciple" to Christ. Perhaps he had been in the crowd when Jesus healed the sick or raised someone from the dead, or maybe he had seen Jesus turn a little boy's lunch into an all-you-can-eat seafood buffet for more than five thousand people. In any case, it is safe to assume he wanted to be associated with a winner, and for the moment Jesus was "in."

In verse 58, though, Jesus punctures this man's bubble. The message is clear. *Association* with Jesus Christ means *identification* with Him and His purposes. In as many words, Jesus lets the man know the truth: Commitment is not based on popularity, the response of the crowd, or merely what we will get out of the relationship. It goes far beyond words and circumstances.

Many Christians are verbally committed to Jesus Christ.

We know the words and the phrases. We are experts at "God talk." Yet, despite the use of the latest Christian buzzwords, I'm not so sure most of us have counted the cost of following Christ on a personal level. You know what I mean—we'd rather have a comfortable Christianity with very few demands.

That's where this man was. He wanted to be a follower of Christ; but he also wanted to be comfortable, to make a nice, safe decision. Jesus cut through his real motivation with the warning that to follow Him was not always going to be a bed of roses. There would be times of suffering and personal sacrifice. Remember, He reminded the man, "foxes have holes" and "birds of the air have nests," but the Son of Man had nothing. Discipleship is much more than verbal commitment!

THE "PROCRASTINATING DISCIPLE"

Verse 59 introduces the second confrontation we want to examine. Jesus challenges this man to "follow Me." This would-be disciple responds, "Permit me first to go and bury my father."

In no uncertain terms, Jesus replies (v. 60), "Allow the dead to bury their own dead; but as for you, go and proclaim everywhere the kingdom of God."

I must admit when I first read these words as a young Christian, I thought this was a horrible thing for Jesus to say to the man. Let's face it. Apparently the poor guy's father was dead, and all he wanted to do was go back home, bury his father, and perhaps take care of some personal business. After he straightened out that crisis he would come and follow Christ. I thought it was a legitimate reason. However, after a closer examination of the text and the language idioms of the time, I discovered that the man's father was probably very much alive. The man was using a colloquialism, a slang expression.

During the time of Christ, older people were often referred to as those who were dying. In other words, the man was really saying, "Allow me to go home and take care of my father *until* he dies."

This interpretation is further underscored by Jesus' reply, "Allow the dead to bury their own dead." Jesus Himself is using a colloquialism. I don't know about you, but where I come from dead people don't bury dead people! I would wager this man knew exactly what Jesus meant: "Your father may be old, but he is not dead. You must get your priorities in order."

It's not that Jesus is against caring for the elderly—He's not. The point of the text is the man's choices and priorities in life, not his father's condition. It is important to care for our families, but that which gives meaning to life is our unreserved and undistracted commitment to follow Christ. Our friend said he wanted to follow Christ, but he wanted to take care of his father first. Jesus would not tolerate this for a moment. Instead, He clearly told this man that his priority must be to go and proclaim the kingdom of God.

Jesus said in Matthew 6:33 that when we put Him first, all of life's concerns have a way of falling into place: "Seek *first* His kingdom and His righteousness, and *all these things* will be added to you" (italics added).

Following Christ is not a series of self-determined, selective options—it is the only option He gives us; and our commitment to follow Him takes priority over everything else in life. We must not procrastinate. Yet that is just what some of us do. We live in a state of procrastination, a sort of "partial obedience." We often use the expression "growth in grace" as a euphemism for our disobedience.

Some of us in the Christian community have become experts at redefining the commandments of God. Jesus told this man that he couldn't put it off. If you are under a "cloud" in your life, and if confusion defines the terms of your direction and coldness describes your sense of purpose, could it be caused partly by procrastination? It's usually not a matter of needing more information on the Christian life; rather, it is that we are not doing and acting on what we already know. We continue to delay our commitment and discipleship.

THE "UNDECIDED DISCIPLE"

In Luke 9:61 we see the third example. I call him the "undecided disciple."

Notice what he says to Jesus: "I will follow You, Lord; but first permit me to say good-bye to those at home." At first glance, you might say there isn't a whole lot of difference between this man and the procrastinating disciple.

There isn't, but notice a slight twist to the procrastination theme. It's called indecision. Jesus' response in verse 62 shows us that that was the man's real problem: "No one, after putting his hand to the plow and looking back, is fit for the kingdom of God." Jesus is not only saying don't put it off, but He's also letting us know that He wants us to make a clear, focused decision.

You can't have it your way and God's way at the same time. Following Jesus Christ is not a merger of other options. It's not an eclectic opportunity; you don't add Jesus to self-centeredness, nor do you add Jesus to *your* perspective and Jesus to *your* philosophy and Jesus to *your* value system. Following Christ is Christ—plus nothing. To follow Christ means to make a single-minded commitment to His cause and call for our lives. Everything else in life is just the arena in which we carry out that commitment and do the will of God.

Jesus uses a powerful analogy to convey the message—a farmer who decides to plow.

Let's say we're back in the 1800s and a local farmer decides he's going to begin plowing the south five acres today, so he hitches up the mules and, determined that his furrows be straight, guides the animals directly toward the big oak tree on the other side of the field. Shortly after he starts he gets distracted. He notices that the fence needs mending. He looks over his shoulder and sees that the chicken coop has to be fixed. Then he looks over the other shoulder and notices that the cows have gotten out of the barn. It doesn't take a genius to realize that, by the time the farmer crosses the field, his furrow is going to be crooked.

We become distracted easily, don't we? It's partly because we find it difficult to make decisions. If we say yes to one thing, we will have to say no to something else. So we keep our options open, trying to get the best from both worlds.

I believe there is another underlying reason for this tendency toward indecision. Many Christians don't believe God has our best interests at heart. Somehow we think we can do a better job of making the decisions and choices for our lives than He can. Perhaps we think we can plea-bargain with God. You know, throw a little of our own philosophy, relationships, and desires into this thing called discipleship and it will all work out—and, as long as we're subtle about it, we can have it all.

No, you and I know we can't have it all (whatever that means). If we're going to follow Christ, we must make a choice. When our relationships, values, and directions conflict with the objective commandments of Scripture, we must cast our way aside and choose for God every time. Whatever it is must be laid aside so that Jesus Christ in His power, wisdom, and glory can live through us. This kind of single-minded commitment both confirms our sense of mission and models a life of purpose and fulfillment to a fractured world.

4
PAYING THE PRICE

Discipleship According to the New Testament

f New Testament discipleship is not merely verbal commitment that can coexist with procrastination and indecision, then what is it?

Jesus answers this question by giving us three crucial ingredients to discipleship in Luke 14:25–35.

Again, historically, this address took place at the peak of Jesus' earthly popularity. People flocked to Him because of all the strange, wonderful things they had heard about Him and His ministry.

They "followed" Him for various reasons and motives. Jesus soon detected that the crowd's perspective needed focusing in a different direction, and He gave them a clear understanding as to just what it would mean to become His true followers.

AN INCOMPARABLE LOVE

The first requirement of New Testament discipleship is *an incomparable love for Christ*. In verse 26 He says, "If anyone comes to Me, and does not *hate* his own father and mother and wife and children and brothers and sisters, yes, and even his own life, *he cannot be My disciple*" (italics added).

This verse is so strong that it borders on the shocking. I would love to have been there when Jesus made that statement. Can you imagine the looks on those faces? The stunned, dumbfounded reaction? I can, because it was exactly my reaction when I first read this verse years ago.

Does Jesus mean a literal *hate?* Does He actually mean that, before we can qualify to be His followers, we must not only reject, but also despise the most treasured and dearest of human relationships? If so, this represents a glaring contradiction of Scripture. We are told throughout the Word of God that we are to love our enemies, our neighbors, and our brothers and sisters in the body of Christ, and to honor and love our parents. What then does Jesus mean by "hate"?

Let me suggest that Jesus is not speaking of a literal hate, but rather of a comparative love. He is making use of hyperbole. A hyperbole is an extravagant exaggeration that represents something as much greater or less, better or worse, than it actually is. It is not lying because there is no intent to deceive. To the contrary, He is using hyperbole to make the truth clear.

You see, our love for Jesus Christ is to be so firm, deep, and intense that when we compare it with the love we have for all of our human relationships, the overwhelming contrast makes what we feel for others to appear as hate.

My wife and I are blessed to have four wonderful children. Often when they were younger I put them to bed in the evening. Part of our bedtime routine usually included a time of singing, reading Bible stories, and prayer.

We've been using the same Bible storybook for years. When our oldest son, Bryan, was about four years old, we'd read the Bible storybook to him so often he virtually had it memorized. What's more, he knew the sequence of the stories and, for whatever reason, would not tolerate our reading one of the stories out of sequence. Usually this little requirement didn't bother me. But one evening I was tired and, I confess, I didn't feel like answering tough questions, especially the persistent ones from an inquisitive four year old. Then, horror of horrors, I discovered that the story for that evening was Abraham offering up Isaac as a sacrifice. *Brother!* I remembered the marathon question-and-answer session Bryan and I had had the last time I read that story, and I wasn't up for it this time.

Plan A was to skip the story and read something that would raise fewer questions, maybe David and Goliath. I tried, but Bryan protested, "Wait a minute, Daddy. Aren't we supposed to read about Abraham killing his son?"

Well, now we're at Plan B, and that was to read the story so fast that the poor little guy didn't have time to even think about questions. Wrong! He stopped me right in the middle of my verbal sprint and asked me the question I feared most, "Daddy, why did God tell Abraham to kill his son?"

It's hard to describe what took place in that little boy's bedroom that evening. I sensed God's presence in a special way, and I realized the Holy Spirit had orchestrated a strategic opportunity to share an important spiritual truth with Bryan. Somehow my tiredness was gone and my impatience suspended for that moment.

I put my arms around my son and said, "Bryan, God told Abraham to offer up Isaac so Abraham could prove to himself that he loved God even more than the most precious possession he had in this life."

His eyes opened wide in wonder, and I continued, "I know you can't fully understand this now. But your mother and I want you to grow up to be a man of God who loves Jesus Christ more than anything else in this world, including your mother and father."

Many of us love our ministries, churches, Bible studies, and Christian activities more than we do the Lord. Discipleship does not begin with activity, or even with knowledge about God and the Christian life. It is first and foremost a love relationship with the Savior of the world, the One who suffered, bled, and died so that we can be cleansed and forgiven of our sins. When we love Him more than anything else in this world, we will obey Him (John 14:23).

IDENTIFICATION WITH THE CROSS

The second requirement of New Testament discipleship is to *fully embrace and identify with the cross of Christ.* Jesus says in Luke 14:27, "Whoever does not carry his own cross and come after Me cannot be My disciple."

This is perhaps one of the most misquoted and/or misapplied verses in the entire Bible. It is often used as a catch-all statement for the suffering and hard times we experience as Christians. It has been my experience and observation, though, that a lot of what we suffer has nothing to do with the cross.

Sometimes we use the "cross" and other spiritual sounding language to disguise areas of neglect or weakness. For example, I have a friend who has a very fruitful ministry. A few years ago he almost lost his wife and family. There was turmoil in the home caused primarily by his absence due to ministry activities. Sometimes he actually said that the friction between him and his wife was the price he had to pay and the *cross* he had to bear because of the call to the ministry. He was dead wrong. His priorities got out of whack and he was too proud to own up to it!

In order to understand what Jesus is saying in Luke 14:27, we must realize He is speaking of the cross both specifically (what it represents) and prophetically (as to His death). The apostle Paul put it this way: "For the word [message] of the cross is foolishness to those who are perishing, but to us who are being saved it is the power of God" (1 Corinthians 1:18).

During the time of Christ the cross represented something brutal and disgusting. It was the Roman way of dealing with criminals. There was nothing respectable about it. It was full of scorn and reproach. That's why Paul said that the message of the cross was foolishness. No one in his right mind would believe that a man who died as a condemned criminal on a Roman cross could be the Savior of the world. Ridiculous! Yet that is precisely what happened!

It cost something to be a follower of Christ during the early days of the church because the crucifixion was still a recent historical event, and new believers were identified with the cross as more than a symbol. In many parts of the world, our brothers and sisters who identify with Christ and His cross today still are being persecuted and even put to death—not for any negligence but merely for their bold, unashamed loyalty to Christ and His cross.

Because here in the United States Christianity has become the unofficial national religion, the cross has been accepted as a respectable symbol of Western civilization. It appears all over the place, on signs, in churches, in jewelry, on bumper stickers— and it's great. You won't have any problems wearing one or even going to church. Does that mean, then, there is no reproach for identifying with the cross in this country? No, if you begin to identify with and proclaim the *message* of the cross, buckle your seat belt, because you're in for a rough ride.

The cross proclaims two very clear messages to us: First, God's holiness and judgment on sin. Second, God's great love for the sinner and forgiveness for his sin. The second one is not too bad, but the first one people find hard to handle. People don't want to be told that they are wrong or that they are sinners. When we humbly seek to live lives that reflect the holiness of God and express His love and forgiveness, sooner or later reproach will find us simply because we are an irritant and nuisance to the sinful self-centeredness of our culture. Yet that's what God has called us to be. Therefore, when the persecution and rejection come, we have the assurance that it has not come as a result of our negligence but as a result of our allegiance to the cross and its message. It is at that point that His cross becomes *our cross.*

We cannot be called His followers unless we are willing to carry the cross.

RELINQUISHED OWNERSHIP

The third requirement for New Testament disciples is to *relinquish ownership.*

Jesus closes out His address on discipleship with the conclusive statement in Luke 14:33: "So then, none of you can be My disciple who does not give up all his own possessions."

This has been a much debated text, and rightly so. It raises the issue of the relationship between the disciple and his possessions. Specifically, the tension is related to the question, "As a follower of Jesus Christ, should I literally own anything in this world?" I know of some Christians who, as a matter of personal conviction, do not own anything. They have no savings account; they own no property; they have no credit cards (that one may not be a bad idea!). They have taken this verse at face value and have sought to order their lives accordingly. I applaud them for it.

However, I see this text a bit differently. I believe Jesus is talking about *ultimate* ownership and not what the world calls ownership. Although we may "own" a house, a car, or a personal computer, the committed disciple realizes that it all belongs to God. Everything has been surrendered to Him, including our family and closest friends. "Our possessions" are both means by which we glorify God and tools by which He accomplishes His purposes through our lives. Our responsibility is to be a faithful steward (manager) of what belongs to Him.

When I was nineteen, I borrowed a friend's car, and through carelessness I ruined the transmission. What struck me was that when I told him what had happened, he said calmly, "Crawford, that's the Lord's car and I'm sure He will provide so it can be fixed." (He did provide—through me—and it cost dearly. That was an expensive lesson for me.) My friend's response, though, taught me a lifelong lesson about letting God handle what He owns. If we have been faithful and responsible managers, there is no need for disappointment when something happens to one of our possessions.

Just before I sat down to write today, our vacuum cleaner died while I was using it. At first, I must admit, I was frustrated because the thing was relatively new and now it's useless. Then I remembered who it belonged to and that He will provide for our needs.

UNENCUMBERED AVAILABILITY

Another issue involved in this matter of relinquishing ownership is that the committed disciple must have an *unencumbered availability*.

When we have acknowledged God's ownership of our possessions, we are emotionally and spiritually free from distractions. If we are attached to our possessions, we are not free to concentrate on eternal things, the things that really matter. We become victims and slaves to the things in our lives. We are, therefore, so mentally or emotionally strapped to our possessions that it is virtually impossible to respond quickly to any direction or leading of the Holy Spirit. I don't know how many times I have been told, "I know the Lord is leading me to serve Him full-time, but I have these debts I must take care of first."

This is not a book on economics, and I don't believe debt, although in most cases unwise, is necessarily sin. However, debt and undue economic preoccupation are effective encumbrances to our full, complete availability to God.

So we see that discipleship is not a matter of verbal commitment, procrastination, or indecision. Rather, dynamic, New Testament discipleship is an incomparable love for Christ, fully embracing and identifying with the cross of Christ, and relinquishing complete ownership of our possessions.

In the next chapter we will look at the most important decision a Christian can make. In fact, this choice not only launches us into a life of effective discipleship, but it also is another essential ingredient in recapturing and maintaining our sense of purpose.

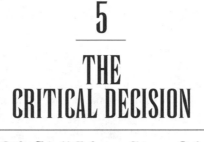

5

THE CRITICAL DECISION

This Will Change Your Life

Purpose in life and a sense of mission, for the Christian, are not simply a matter of desire or even of having the right understanding of the Christian life and of discipleship. If they were, this book would be unnecessary. We know, though, that truth alone has never produced change or brought a sense of purpose to even one life.

One of the major problems of Christianity today is that Christians *know* so much but *do* so little. Information and even "the correct theology" have been mistaken for dynamic, refreshing, life-changing Christianity—but that doesn't compute.

A right knowledge about God and His Word does not necessarily translate to a right walk or a vital relationship with God. Some of the most "biblically sound" churches I know have about as much life as the city morgue.

Though there is nothing wrong with emotions, I am not talking about emotionalism or any sort of superficial "Mary Poppins" approach to the Christian life. I am talking about a life that reflects the supernatural, victorious life which is ours through Jesus Christ—Christianity overflowing with joy, purpose, and power. This can be the experience of every Christian.

How do we get there from here? What's missing?

Two important links connect our knowledge about God and His Word to effective Christianity. The first is what I call the critical decision, and the second is living daily under the control of the Holy Spirit. Since a later chapter in this book deals with the ministry of the Holy Spirit, this chapter will be devoted to the first link, the critical decision.

MAKING THE DECISION

It has been my painful observation through nineteen years of public ministry that the vast majority of Christians have never made this decision. The fruitless and aimless Christianity that has become the norm for so many Christians bears this out. Without this decision, there can be no sustained sense of purpose. Making the decision will make all the difference in the world.

What is the decision?

Simply stated, it is

To decide, once and for all, as an act of the will, to dedicate all that we have and are to Jesus Christ.

"Wait a minute! I thought, when I received Jesus Christ as my Savior and Lord, that one decision forever settled both the issues of my salvation and my dedication to Him."

I am sure that for some Christians, when they received Christ it was a full, all-out commitment to Him. Yet I am more convinced this is not the experience of most Christians. Usually, a period of time elapses between our trusting Christ for the forgiveness of sin and our realizing we cannot live the Christian life in our own strength, based upon our own agenda. At that point we must make the critical decision regarding complete dedication to Jesus Christ. For some this is a gradual decision. For others it is a more historic, crisis-oriented choice. Nevertheless, the decision must be made. The alternative is to be trapped in the crowded sea of spiritual mediocrity.

THE ANATOMY OF THE DECISION

The apostle Paul gives us the anatomy of this decision in Romans 12:1–2:

Therefore I urge you, brethren, by the mercies of God, to present your bodies a living and holy sacrifice, acceptable to God, which is your spiritual service of worship. And do not be conformed to this world, but be transformed by the renewing of your mind, that you may prove what the will of God is, that which is good and acceptable and perfect.

The central message of these two verses is a call to a life totally dedicated to Jesus Christ. However, this one decision is given to us in three parts, three steps.

MOTIVATION FOR MAKING THE DECISION

Before we get to the three steps, though, we need to look briefly at the motivation for making the decision. This is introduced by the little word *therefore* at the beginning of verse one. At first glance, we could be tempted to glide over this word and get to the meat of the passage. Yet this little grammatical helper ("therefore") introduces *why* we should dedicate our lives to Christ in the first place. In the previous eleven chapters the apostle Paul has been building his case and laying the groundwork for the punch line in Romans 12:1–2.

In chapters 1–3 he lets us know, in no uncertain terms, that anyone who does not have a relationship with Christ is eternally lost. In the latter part of chapter 3 and through chapter 5, he powerfully presents Jesus Christ, God's solution to our condemnation. In chapters 6 through 8 Paul tells us about the Holy Spirit, who is God's wonderful provision for overcoming sin and temptation. Finally, in chapters 9 through 11, the apostle describes the spiritual heritage we have as a result of our commitment to Christ.

That brings us to Romans 12:1 where Paul makes the dramatic transition: "Therefore I urge you . . ." The argument is irresistible and the message is overwhelmingly clear. It's as if he were saying, "On the basis of God's sacrificial, eternal love for you through His Son, it only makes sense to give your all to Him!" He then tells us how to do it. The "how-to" is summarized in the three dominant verbs: "present" (verse 1), "be conformed" (verse 2), and "be transformed" (also verse 2). By the way, decisions should produce a change of life (verbs). It is not simply an appreciation of who we are in Christ (noun) but what we do (verb) and how we live (verb) as a result of what we know that produces both change and impact for Christ and His cause.

Step 1: Presenting Your Body

The first step is to "present your body as a living sacrifice." The verb *present* in the Greek text is in the aorist tense. This means a historic action, a point of reference. It's clear. Paul says make the decision and settle it once and for all. Make the monumental decision that will forever govern all your choices and your direction in life.

Notice what he says to present as a "living sacrifice": our bodies. I often wondered why the apostle said to present to God our bodies. Why didn't he say to give God our activities, or our time, or our money, or our minds? Why body? Then it dawned on me one day that our body is the visible representation of everything that we were, are, and ever will be. If Jesus Christ has our body, then He has the sum total of all that we are. He has it all, and that's what He wants.

The story is told of David Brainerd, the famed missionary to the Native Americans of the eighteenth century, who one day was speaking to a small group of people. As he was speaking, the chief, evidently under great conviction, interrupted Brainerd. With his horse in tow, he said, "The chief gives his horse to God."

He sat down and Brainerd continued to preach. It wasn't enough. The chief interrupted a second time and determined to give the most treasured of his possessions: "The chief gives his headdress to God."

Once again he sat down and Brainerd continued to preach. Finally, still deeply disturbed, the chief jumped to his feet and said, "The chief has nothing else of value to give to God, so the chief presents himself to God!"

How many of us are like that Indian chief, giving bits and pieces of our lives, but not the all-important gift of ourselves? We opt for an à la carte Christianity; you know, pick and choose whatever happens to be tasteful and satisfying to our spiritual appetite at the time. *We* maintain control and dictate to God what He can or cannot do. We reserve the right to choose the areas of our lives He can control. We post "no trespassing" signs over certain sections and "limited access" warnings over other areas.

We are living in an era of what I call "recreational Christianity," the kind of Christianity that reduces God to a personal valet, catering to *my* needs,—the kind of Christianity that helps me to feel good, be happy, and be successful. We are then "dedicated" to Him as long as things are going our way, we have money in the bank, and we have our health. This recreational Christianity has produced self-enslavement, perverted theology, and a church whose only sense of purpose and direction is determined by itself.

In the midst of our "evangelical self-determinism," God shouts through the pen of the apostle Paul, "Take your hands off your life and present your bodies a living, holy sacrifice."

"Present" is only the first verb. There's more.

Step 2: Declaring Your Allegiance

The second verb has to do with our relationship to this world's system. The opening clause of verse 2 says, "Do not be *conformed* to this world"; or, as the Phillips version puts it: "Don't let the world around you squeeze you into its mold." Conformity to the world has to do with the issue of allegiance and control. To be surrendered to the lordship of Jesus Christ means to follow His directions and not the dictates of this world's system. That is why the definition of *worldliness* is much more than merely doing what the world does. It is, in fact, doing what the world does *because the world tells you to do it*. It is all a matter of who you're listening to.

John says, "Do not love the world nor the things in the world" (1 John 2:15). The key word here is *love*. John clearly states that worldliness is an internal attitude of allegiance to this world's system—again, not necessarily activities, but allegiance (love).

Christians do many of the same things non-Christians do. We own homes; we drive cars; we work at the same places; we enjoy some of the same entertainment. What's the difference? It is that as Christians we do these things because God gives us the privilege to do them and to enjoy life. If we did them because of the pressures and expectations of society, we would be worldly.

Why do you live where you live? Why do you own the kind of car you own? Why do you wear the kind and style of clothes you wear? Why do you go to certain places? Why do you enjoy a particular kind of entertainment? Is it because of the expectations (sometimes subtle) of your environment? Is it a desire to be approved and accepted by your peers? If the answer is yes, you qualify for the label "worldly."

However, if your daily life choices are influenced primarily by your relationship with God and His Word, then you definitely are not worldly. Again, it is who and what influences you, not necessarily what you do. In that sense we are not to be "conformed to the world."

Of course, many of the choices we make don't fall readily into one of these two categories. If your employer requires you to wear a suit, you don't need to search the Scriptures to see if wearing a suit to work would be inappropriate worldly conformance. That's a neutral cultural element. Many personal preferences also fall into the category of morally neutral choices. What colors do you like to wear, and do you care more about safety or reliability when you buy a car?

Christians have freedom in such cases, but that doesn't remove those choices from the realm of godly decision making. It's possible to spend more than you need to on that suit for the office because you want to make a particular impression. That's pride, and God says a lot about that. It's also possible to enjoy the wrong kinds of entertainment and justify it as part of modern culture. But only God can judge motives—outward appearances don't show *why* a person has made a particular choice. If your morally significant choices conform to God's Word and your motives and attitude are right in all your decision making, then you are not worldly.

Step 3: Committing to Action

The cure for worldliness is found in the third verb: "Be *transformed* by the renewing of your mind." The only way to flesh out our dedication to Jesus Christ is through a renewed mind.

To put it another way: Transformation is the product of what we think about.

Solomon said, "As a man thinks so is he." There is a direct relationship between our thoughts and actions. What a person dwells on, he eventually will act upon. Even if a person is a masterful hypocrite, eventually his actions will betray him and reveal his thoughts, and he will be "caught."

In the name of "open-mindedness," some Christians have no problem reading pornography, attending questionable movies, and exposing their minds to that which is diametrically opposed to, and ultimately damaging to, their walk with Christ. Christians should not live in a cocoon and we should be informed of the issues facing our world, but there are some things we must not allow to occupy our minds. I'm not going to list them. I have a sneaking suspicion you know clearly what they are. To quote the United Negro College Fund slogan, "A mind is a terrible thing to waste."

If obedience to truth produces change, and if it is true that what a person dwells on he will eventually act upon, then the greatest thing we can do is to fill our minds with the Word of God. Meditation on the Word of God will not only protect us from worldliness, but it also will preserve and protect our convictions and fuel our sense of purpose.

David said in Psalm 119:11, "Your word I have treasured in my heart, that I may not sin against You." I am convinced that we often fall into sin because we neglect consistent study and application of God's Word. It is precious. It is powerful. It is eternal. It is our guide to victory in this life. If we neglect it, we are doomed.

How much time do you spend reading and memorizing the Scriptures? Do you have a daily habit of reading the Word of God? Are you struggling with sin in your life? Is there very little peace, if any, in your life? Come back to the compass. Pour the Word of God into your heart and soul. Make Bible study a priority, an indispensable part of your daily routine, and you will have a powerful weapon with which to combat the barrage of mental missiles hurled at you daily.

"Wait a minute," you say, "I've tried that before, and it's hard to do. Besides, I'm busy and other things always squeeze out the time set aside for Bible study."

Admittedly, preserving that daily time for Bible study and prayer is one of the most difficult challenges facing all of us, but we must make it our top priority. Literally, our spiritual lives depend on it. I hear someone saying, "We must not be legalistic about this." Legalism, no. Decision and discipline, yes.

If the motive for Bible study is to prove to God and others that we are spiritual because of what we do, we are legalistic. However, if the motive is to know God and His will for our lives through the disciplined study of His Word and through prayer, we are not legalistic. It's all a matter of motive—not simply activity.

DISCIPLINE IS THE KEY

The key word is discipline. We must be willing to lay aside our interests and agenda to be able to give God and His Word top billing in our lives. It's a struggle, but anything worthwhile involves struggle. In fact, God has infused all of life with the basic principle that out of struggle will come strength.

The principle is powerfully illustrated in nature. The eagle is a prime example. The mother teaches the baby to fly by placing it on her back and soaring over the valley. She throws the little one off her back, and just before it falls to certain doom she swoops it up to safety. She repeats this performance until the little creature can fly solo. God placed in that bird the intuitive principle that if it struggles long enough, it will fly.

A man noticed he had a monarch butterfly cocoon dangling from his kitchen windowsill. He eagerly awaited the day this beautiful butterfly would make its grand entrance into the world. One day he saw the cocoon shaking. "This is it," he said, "we're going to have a birthday." In his enthusiasm, wanting to help with the "delivery," he got a razor and made a slight incision in the cocoon. After the butterfly emerged, it died. Only in the butterfly's struggle to break out of the cocoon could it gain the strength it needed to survive.

God honors our disciplined commitment to study and

apply His Word to our lives. In this daily discipline we will gain the spiritual strength not only to survive but also to be victorious.

God has given us the strength for the journey through Christ. Everything we need is in Him. However, before those resources can be released to us and through our lives to others, we must make the critical decision: We must decide to surrender all that we have and are to Him. Acknowledge Him today as the Lord of your entire life and affairs. Then demonstrate that commitment through the consistent study and application of His Word.

In the next chapter we'll examine the personal benefits of a life that is surrendered to the lordship of Christ and His will for our lives.

6

PURSUING A LIFE OF PURPOSE

Personal Benefits of a Surrendered Life

N ot long ago I went to Nassau, in the Bahamas, to fulfill a speaking engagement. The trip came at the tail end of a grueling travel schedule packed with meetings, speaking, and other responsibilities.

I foolishly had not paced myself; so, because of a lack of rest and exercise, I was both physically and emotionally drained. In fact, while walking along the beach the morning after I arrived in Nassau, I prayed, "Lord, I am so wiped out that I don't know whether this thing called ministry is really worth it." Any sense of mission and purpose had worn thin.

No sooner had I uttered that prayer than I looked up and saw people frantically running down the beach. Something awful must have happened! I picked up my pace too. When I reached the group, they had surrounded a man lying on the ground. Apparently he had been drinking and decided to go for a swim, then became disoriented and drowned. Someone attempted CPR, but it was no use. He was gone. The crowd slowly dispersed. Eventually I, too, walked away. A thousand thoughts flooded my mind. I wondered who the man was and where he came from, but the question that bothered me most was, What about his eternal destiny?

Then I remembered my prayer, and I realized God had responded. "Yes, Crawford, this thing called ministry is worth it."

I was overwhelmed with praise to God for calling me to invest my life in sharing the good news of Christ's death, burial, and resurrection for the sins of the world. Despite my physical weariness, I once again saw clearly what a wonderful privilege it is to fulfill His purpose for my life. Though sadly burdened for this man and his family, my sense of mission was strengthened. I renewed my determination to pursue God's purpose and will for my life.

Every once in a while God has to do something drastic to remind us whose we are and whose mission we are on. The clutter and clamor of life, crowded schedules, weariness, and pressure make it difficult at times to hear and heed God's direction. Or, we get so used to making our own choices and decisions that we don't want to do otherwise. Often, that's not so much an active rebellion as it is acquiescence to circumstances or expectations. Then God interrupts us with the message of the lordship of Christ: As Lord of our lives, Jesus Christ has the authority to lead and direct us.

And lead and direct He does! I don't mean in some general sense; I mean in a specific way. God has a plan for His children. He has something specific for each individual to do and a place for each one to be. As we listen and obey the voice of God in the daily direction of our lives, we will experience a supernatural sense of mission and purpose. This is what is meant by living in and doing the will of God.

Some people say there is no such thing as a "personal will of God." They stress that anything a Christian does—as long as it is not sinful—is the will of God. God's will for our lives is contained in the Bible and that's it, they say.

I strongly disagree. Certainly, God's will is contained in His Word, but throughout the Scriptures there is abundant proof that God leads His children concerning life choices. (See Jonah; Proverbs 3:5–6; and Acts 13:1–3; 16:6–10.) He did it in Bible days, and every evidence indicates that this divine direction has not ceased. Quite the contrary. Any Christian who does not yield to the clear leading of the Holy Spirit that is confirmed by and conformed to the Word of God is living in sinful disobedience to God. Remember, the purpose of surrender to the lordship of Christ is to "prove what the will of God is, that which is good and acceptable and perfect" (Romans 12:2b).

Of course God expects us to use our minds and the wisdom that comes through His Word and through our experiences, but we do not rely on our minds and past experiences. We trust Him for the direction. Do we then pray about what color sock we should wear, or how we comb our hair, or which way to cut the grass? No. We use our heads.

However, when it comes to the way we live our lives, the direction of our lives, and the decisions related to our effectiveness for Christ and His cause, we must not settle for anything less than God's best. It is better to err on the side of seeming to be too dependent on God than to allow ourselves to become presumptuous.

FINDING GOD'S WILL

Although this is not a chapter on how to find God's will, it may help if I make a few observations along that line.

First, you must *realize that God is not trying to hide His will from you.* If we want to know God's will for our lives, it will become clear. In fact, He wants us to know His will more than we do. He is not playing hide-and-seek with us. First Corinthians 2:12–16 gives us the primary condition for discovering God's will: living in fellowship with God (with our sins confessed to God and living in the power of the Holy Spirit).

Second, we must *go to the Word of God.* God will never lead us to do anything that contradicts His Word. Be careful. Don't let your desire to do something cause you to make the Bible say more or less than it says. It's amazing how we can use the Scriptures to justify what we want to do. Let God speak for Himself through His Word.

Third, *check the circumstances and patterns in your life.* Often, God will so orchestrate the circumstances and events in our lives that it is fairly obvious what He wants us to do. Again, be careful not to read too much into events or circumstances.

Fourth, you must *trust God to lead you through prayer.* God not only hears us through prayer, but He also responds to us because of prayer. Have you prayed about that decision? Have you asked God to show you what He wants you to do? He promised that He would. Sometimes we don't know God's will simply because we have not taken the time to ask Him ("You do not have because you do not ask," says James 4:2).

Fifth, *solicit the counsel of wise, godly people* (Proverbs 12:15). Don't look for those who will tell you what you want to hear. Seek out balanced, objective people. Listen carefully to their advice. Put it in the "mix," and pray over it.

Finally, *make the decision, and don't look back.* If you have gone through this process with a sincere heart and a desire to know God's will, you can make a confident decision. If you have taken the time to listen to God carefully, don't procrastinate in making your decision. Impetuous choices are a sign of presumption and impatience. Procrastination, however, is a sign of unbelief. If the Lord tells you to wait, wait. A good friend of mine says, "The only thing worse than waiting on God is wishing that you had!" On the other hand, if God tells you to move, go for it!

What happens to us when we commit ourselves to knowing and doing the will of God? What will our lives look like? Colossians 1:9–12 gives us the answer:

> For this reason also, since the day we heard of it, we have not ceased to pray for you and to ask that you may be filled with the knowledge of His will in all spiritual wisdom and understanding, so that you will walk in a manner worthy of the Lord, to please Him in all respects, bearing fruit in every good work and increasing in the knowledge of God; strengthened with all power, according to His glorious might, for the attaining of all steadfastness and patience; joyously giving thanks to the Father, who has qualified us to share in the inheritance of the saints in Light.

In this great prayer there is one central focus: to "be filled with the knowledge of His will." Paul did not pray for these Christians to be well known or even successful. He prayed they would know God's will. He fully realized that an understanding of, and a commitment to, the will of God is the essence of purposeful Christianity. Some wonderful things happen to us.

TRANSFORMED CHARACTER

One of them is a *character transformation.* The passage says we will "walk in a manner worthy of the Lord." This refers to who we are and how we live. When we are committed to doing God's will, who we are and what we do reflects God's agenda. Our relationship with Him and His purposes will influence what we do. The word *worthy* literally means of "equal weight." In other words, our relationship with God gives us all of the rights and privileges to serve as His representatives in this world. What a sobering thought! Since we are His representatives, we don't want to be disqualified because of disobedience.

The story is told that Alexander the Great one day met with his lieutenants to discuss war strategy. One of them revealed that he was having some difficulty with one of his men. Alexander sent for this young soldier. When he arrived, the great general asked the young man what his name was. The soldier responded, "Oddly enough, my name is Alexander."

In a furor the general said, "Either you change your name or you change your conduct!"

If we are related to the God of the universe, we will want to demonstrate it by our obedience to His will.

GOD'S RESOURCES

Our knowledge and commitment to the will of God also will provide us with God's resources to face life's challenges. This sustaining promise is given in verse 11: "Strengthened with all power, according to His glorious might, for the attaining of all steadfastness and patience." Think of it! All of heaven's resources are at our disposal when we yield ourselves to do the will of God. He gives us the strength needed to do and to endure.

Karen and I had a daughter who died two hours after birth. The baby came two weeks before the due date. Unfortunately, I was out of town on a quick trip at the time. When I received word that Karen had been taken to the hospital and that the baby had died, I was crushed. Hurt, anger, and frustration raged within me. On the flight home I stared out the window with tears rolling down my face wondering why God would allow this to happen. Why did our baby come two weeks early? Why did it have to happen while I was away? I was overwhelmed with both guilt and anger, anger with God because I felt this whole thing was unfair and that He had let me down, and guilt because I was not there when the dearest person in my life really needed me. I was flirting with bitterness.

Our pastor met me at the airport and took me to the hospital. When we arrived, one of the nurses let me see our little girl. Although she was dead, she appeared to have a smile on her face. *She is with the Lord,* I told myself. I then walked into Karen's room. We embraced, prayed, and cried together. Through her tears she said, "Honey, for whatever reason, God has decided to take our baby home to be with Him."

Later that evening I got down on my knees and poured my heart out to God in prayer. I confessed my anger and frustration to Him. I told Him He did not owe me an answer or an explanation. My life belongs to Him, and if this is what it takes to make us more like Him and to be His obedient children, then by faith I accept and thank Him for it. I then asked Him to use the death of our baby for His glory, and to give us the strength to face the days and weeks ahead.

As soon as I prayed both Karen and I experienced a sense of peace and strength that can only be explained by God's supernatural intervention. Yes, we still feel sadness over our loss, but we have experienced God's strength to endure. We have learned that God always gives us what we need to do what He calls us to do and to go through what He allows to come our way.

GRATEFUL ATTITUDE

There is one final thing. When we are committed to knowing and doing God's will, we will have *grateful attitudes.* This is introduced in the last word of verse 11 and in verse 12 of Colossians 1: "Joyously giving thanks to the Father, who has qualified us to share in the inheritance of the saints in Light."

An understanding of our part in God's program for the world should cause us to explode with joy and appreciation. He has not only forgiven us and delivered us from the penalty of our sin, but He also has given us an inheritance, the legacy of His will.

Christianity is not a sick, sour lifestyle meant to be tolerated at best. It is an incredible, adventurous journey in which redeemed, forgiven people live like their Master, the Lord Jesus Christ. We are those who face life's struggles and challenges with joy because we know the "rest of the story." We are on the winning side. We have an inheritance that no one can take away. Therefore, out of gratitude to God, we want to do His will!

When is the last time you sat down and recounted what God has done for you? Have you thought lately about where you'd be today if it were not for Jesus Christ? Gratitude is the product of remembering God's unfailing track record in our lives. When we are truly grateful, we will be moved to submit our wills to His. Gratitude is an important link in recapturing and maintaining our sense of purpose.

Gratitude fuels our desire to obey, especially when it comes to doing the thing dearest and nearest to the heart of God. We'll take a look at what that is in the next chapter.

7

UNDERSTANDING OUR MARCHING ORDERS

The Difference Between an Institution and a Movement

T he primary motivation for doing the will of God is gratitude—a heart filled with praise for the forgiveness of sin, for our acceptance into the family of God, and for the wonderful inheritance we have in Him. I cannot think of anything more motivating! We should be especially excited about sharing this life-changing message with everyone we come in contact with.

Bill Bright, the founder and president of Campus Crusade for Christ, often says, "If coming to know Christ is the greatest thing that has happened to you, it only makes sense that the greatest thing you can do for someone else is to introduce them to Him." It's that simple.

THE MOTIVATION

God intends for His children to channel their gratitude into faithful, loyal obedience to Christ. This attitude is crisply addressed in 2 Corinthians 5:14–15:

> For the love of Christ controls us, having concluded this, that one died for all, therefore all died; and He died for all, so that they who live might no longer live for themselves, but for Him who died and rose again on their behalf.

Realizing Christ died for our sin and accepting that death forever changes our attitudes about life and about ourselves. We cannot be selfish. We must obey Him; we must tell the liberating message of the Cross to the world.

THE RESPONSIBILITY

That's the motivation. The command is objective, something we do because we have been directed by the sovereign Lord of history to do it. Every Christian has been given the task of helping to fulfill the Great Commission of Jesus Christ. No matter where God positions you in life, He expects you to use that position as a platform to reach and disciple as many people as possible. Again, this is not an option; it is God's will for our lives. Obedience is the key to recapturing our sense of purpose.

It is my conviction that many of us have lost our sense of purpose because we have become sidetracked. First, we focus on many good and noble Christian activities and neglect the most important thing, the reason Christ came to earth: "to seek and to save the lost." Bible studies, fellowship meetings, worship services, church building programs, and prayer meetings are all important, but they are not a substitute for the proclamation of the good news of Jesus Christ. The good often becomes the enemy of the best. *Everything* we do as Christians must feed our two principle objectives: worshiping God and witnessing for Him.

The second way we are sidetracked is through confusion as to what we are to be about—in other words, what our mission is. We may accept the fact that the world needs the opportunity to trust Christ as Savior and Lord, but we do not accept our personal responsibility in making it possible. We place the burden on the shoulders of the paid Christian professionals, the pastors, the evangelists, and the missionaries. We pray for them. We give them our money. We bring our friends to hear them. To be sure, we need to do all of this, but what about us? The entire body of Christ has ownership in the responsibility of fulfilling the Great Commission. No one is excluded.

THE CALL

We need to clarify our responsibility in order to understand our marching orders. Therefore, let's take a closer look at what we are called to do, what we are commanded to do, and to whom we are commissioned to do it. In so doing, we will activate our sense of purpose. When we know what we are, we are well on our way to doing what we are placed here to do. Understanding gives reason to action.

Jesus stressed this point to His disciples in Matthew 16:13–18. He wanted them to know that they were called to be a part of something much bigger than any one of them.

The disciples had been with Jesus for perhaps two years by this time. They had seen a lot and been through a lot together. Now their Master takes them on a strategic retreat and begins their time together by raising what, on the surface, appears to be a fairly innocent question. He simply asks, "Who do people say that the Son of Man is?" (v. 13). Today we would call that a market-sensitive question: "What are they saying about Me on Main Street?"

WHO JESUS IS

Many students of the Scriptures believe that Jesus was baiting His followers and setting them up for Peter's revelation a few verses later. I agree. However, I also believe Jesus wanted them to discuss what the people had to say about Him and His ministry.

In this industry phase of Christianity that we are in (in which marketing considerations rather than the Word of God drives ministry), all too often we are more concerned about what the Christian world says about our ministry than about what God says or the effect on those who stand to benefit from it most, the unbelievers.

It's not how great a job we think we are doing that matters. What are unbelievers saying about our lives and witness? What are they saying about us on our jobs? What are they saying about us on campus? What are they saying about us in our community? We represent Jesus Christ. As unbelievers examine our lives, who do they say that the Son of Man is?

The disciples answered the question in Matthew 16:14: "Some say John the Baptist; and others, Elijah; but still others, Jeremiah, or one of the prophets." Although the people obviously caught the prophetic edge to His ministry, they missed the point. Close, but no prize. This prompted Jesus to ask His disciples, "But who do *you* say that I am?" (verse 15).

Peter's response reveals the cornerstone and essence of what we believe as Christians. Yet it's more than just what we believe. Throughout the centuries men and women literally have put their lives on the line for this confession. And rightly so—to deny it is to reject what makes Christianity Christianity.

Notice carefully what Peter said in verse 16: "You are the Christ, the Son of the living God." Bulls-eye! Unlike "the people," Peter did not miss the point. The core of his confession is the expression, "the Christ." *Christ* is the New Testament Greek word for the Old Testament word *Messiah*. Both these expressions mean "the Anointed One."

The Jews had longed for the day when Messiah would come to establish His kingdom. They eagerly awaited that day. However, when He did come, they rejected Him.

Notice, too, that Peter uses the definite article *the*. This is a statement of the authentic, singular nature of Jesus' position and person. In other words, He is the one and only Messiah. There is none other and there never will be another. He is the everlasting Messiah, God in flesh (John 1:14; Philippians 2:6–11). "Son of the living God" is a descriptive statement of His deity and authority. He is God. He has all of the authority and power to accomplish His purposes in this world (Matthew 28:18).

I don't know about you, but this incredible revelation overwhelms me. It moves me to worship the King of kings and Lord of lords, Jesus Christ!

But watch this.

THE CHURCH

In Matthew 16:17 Jesus reminds Peter where this revelation came from: "Flesh and blood did not reveal this to you, but My Father who is in heaven." In verse 18 He identifies the new movement He is inaugurating: "Upon this rock I will build My church; and the gates of Hades will not overpower it." Peter's name comes from the same root word as the word *rock*. However, *Peter* comes from *petros*, which means "small stone." *Rock* comes from *petra* which means "large rock" or "bedrock." The rock referred to here is the *confession* of Peter: "You are the Christ, the Son of the living God."

The church referred to here is not brick and mortar. The church is comprised of all those who have placed their faith in Jesus Christ as Savior and Lord. We are the church. It is the church that has been guaranteed ultimate victory because we have a sure foundation: "The Christ, the Son of the living God." That has been our calling card throughout the ages, and we must continue to be known as those who possess a passionate commitment to "the Christ." Any time that commitment has been eclipsed by fads, popular issues, or various tangents, the church has become anemic and without direction or hope for the world.

This is also true on an individual level. Jesus Christ is our life. When we wander from Him and lose our passion for Him, we too throw away our direction and impact. He is calling us back to Himself. Remember the rock. Remember the foundation.

Jesus Christ is building His church on this sure foundation. Look again at the verb, "I will *build* My church." This is His chief objective until He returns. Jesus Christ is calling people to Himself from every tribe, tongue, and nation, people from every conceivable background: wealthy, poor, middle class, urban, suburban, rural. He is calling all kinds of people: "blue bloods," outcasts, the respectable, the morally reprehensible, the powerful, the weak. They are coming to Christ and receiving His love, forgiveness, and hope. All these are members of His body, the church. We are one in Him and peers because of the Cross.

A MOVEMENT

The church as pictured here is an aggressive movement. Look at what Jesus says: "The gates of hell shall not prevail against it" (Matthew 16:18 KJV). This is a powerful analogy. The key to capturing Jesus' point is noticing the word *gates*. During the time of Christ, the gates of a city symbolically represented the strength of the city. A city with strong gates was secure and safe from the attacks of the enemy. That's why, upon capturing a city, invading armies would remove the gates from their hinges, announcing to the world that the strength and security of the city had been broken.

The church is an invading movement in the world. We are going against the forces of darkness, yet Jesus Himself promises that the "gates of hell" will not be able to withstand the aggressive onslaught of this movement. We have been guaranteed victory.

Historically, the church often has allowed itself to be cornered into a reactionary or responding posture. That's not what God intended. We are called to be initiators and pacesetters for righteousness. We set the agenda for godliness and holiness of life and practice. We offer the world the only viable alternative to loneliness, hopelessness, and enslavement to sin. We offer God's point of view on the issues of our times. More than that, we creatively take every opportunity to give men and women a chance to place their faith in the living Lord of history, Jesus Christ.

Characteristics of a Movement

The church is not an organization, neither is it an institution in the modern sense of the word. It is a *movement*. Organizations and institutions exist primarily for the perpetuation of a program, and/or to service a need. There are significant differences between an institution and a movement.

At least five distinguishing features characterize a movement:

- First, a strong charismatic leader
- Second, a clear mission
- Third, a flexibility of methodology
- Fourth, the enlistment and mobilization of the masses to accomplish the mission
- Fifth, the obvious commitment on the part of the members to make it happen

As a movement, the church embodies these five features. Our leader is Jesus Christ. Our mission is the fulfillment of the Great Commission.

Because we are flexible in our methods, "We become all things to all people, so that we may win some."

As we share the gospel, those who believe become members of the movement, and they are charged with the same mission.

Of course, the commitment of the believers is in direct proportion to the success of the movement. Sometimes movements die. As I mentioned, the church is guaranteed victory. In that sense our movement will never die. That's not true on a local level, though. Sad to say, many dead local churches can be found. They have become diverted, or discouraged, or simply complacent. The fire has gone out. Fervent prayer has dwindled down. Few people witness for Christ. As a result, few new converts are made.

Why does this happen? There are many reasons, I suppose. However, oddly enough, success seems to be one of the primary causes for the death of a particular church within the movement. With success comes a tendency to relax and coast a bit. We easily allow ourselves to become consumed with a false sense of security and importance. We look around us and say, "Hey, we're doing much better than the other churches and ministries in the area." We forget what got us "there," and we manage to attribute Spirit-produced results to human ability and effort.

How a Church Dies

The death of a church is a slow, painful process. I've identified three phases.

First, the church begins as a movement, fully committed to the five distinguishing features. Then, because of the members' faithful obedience to Christ and His cause, God in His grace grants success. The church grows both spiritually and numerically. Before long, rejoicing degenerates into pride and a desire to keep the operation moving. No more risks. You don't want to jeopardize what *you* have built.

Enter the second phase. Congratulations! The movement has now become an organization. On the surface, it's not always easy to distinguish a movement from an organization, but there is one telltale sign. An organization focuses on the perpetuation of the program. Flexibility and Spirit-led creativity are virtually nonexistent. Bureaucracy reigns supreme. When a process or program is questioned a typical response is, "We've always done it this way, and this is what we are comfortable with."

Unless there is a touch of revival, the third phase is unavoidable. The movement becomes a monument. A monument is a statement of past success and significance. The people now talk about what used to be. They reminisce about the "glory days." There is no vision for the future. There is no "building of the church." The movement of that church has died.

This is also true on an individual level. Has the fire gone out of your life? Are you trusting God to use you to help build His church? We are part of the movement, and as such we must play our part in accomplishing the mission of that movement.

Let's take a look in the next chapter at what the mission of the movement is and what we are commanded to do.

8

THE MISSION AND THE COMMAND

Compassion and the Great Commission

 atthew 28:18–20 is the clear, classic passage on the mandate of the church, the Great Commission. Jesus says,

> All authority has been given to Me in heaven and on earth. Go therefore and make disciples of all the nations, baptizing them in the name of the Father and the Son and the Holy Spirit, teaching them to observe all that I commanded you; and lo, I am with you always, even to the end of the age.

WHAT WE ARE TO DO

This Great Commission begins with a statement of Christ's authority (verse 18), and it concludes with the assurance of His abiding presence (verse 20). In between we are told what to do (verse 19a) and how to do it ("baptizing," verse 19b, and "teaching," verse 20). For our purposes here, I want to comment on what we have been commanded to do.

Verse 19 begins: "Go therefore and make disciples of all the nations." Let me make three observations about this statement as it relates to the Great Commission.

The Command of the Commission

First, observe that the *command* in this verse is not the word *go* but the expression "make disciples." This is the imperative mood, a command. To "make disciples" is the Great Commission. God's purpose through our lives and witness is to produce faithful *reproducing* followers of Christ. Notice He did not say to "make converts," or even to "make believers," but to "make disciples." There is a significant difference. As we saw earlier, a disciple is an obedient follower of Christ. We seem to have a lot of converts and believers, but where are the disciples?

We need to trust God to use us, not only to lead people to a saving knowledge of Christ, but also to nurture them toward maturity so they can do the same (2 Timothy 2:2). This is not the "Great Suggestion." This is a command that requires our obedience.

The Arena for Carrying Out the Commission

Second, observe the *arena* for the fulfillment of the Great Commission: the places of our daily activities. "Go therefore" in the Greek text is what is known as a circumstantial participle. It could have been translated "while you go" or "as you are going . . ." Making disciples is to be part of everything we do. Throughout the course of our day we look to God to use us to introduce people to His Son. Wherever we go we look for those divine appointments—at the mall, on the job, at school, in the community. Wherever we are we can find candidates for the kingdom, people whose hearts have been prepared to hear and receive the message. The question is, Are we ready and willing to deliver that message?

The Scope of the Commission

Third, the Great Commission is universal in its *scope.* We are to make disciples of "all the nations." The word *nation* is the word *ethnos.* We get the English word *ethnic* from this word. It has to do, not so much with the literal nations of the world, but with the *people* of the world. Every culture and people group in the world must be given the opportunity to say yes to Jesus Christ. We cannot be satisfied by simply reaching "our own." The world is our own. Every Christian is responsible to reach out beyond his own cultural and racial setting.

We must *pray* for the spread and penetration of the gospel around the world. We must *give* of our resources for the worldwide fulfillment of the Great Commission. We must personally be willing to *go* in order for the world to hear. However, there is a certain hypocrisy among many American Christians, isn't there? I mean, we attend world mission conferences and become enthusiastic supporters of the needs in "Otherlands," and we catch a vision and burden for those people. Somehow, though, we seem to have a hard time hurdling the cultural and racial barriers in our own country.

No, it's not an either-or situation. It's both-and. We must reach the entire world, including where we live. By the year 2010 the U.S.A. will be majority minority; that is, the minority populations combined will then outnumber white America for the first time in recent history. Couple this with the incredible number of international students studying at our universities and you will recognize that we have an ideal opportunity to help fulfill the Great Commission.

What about you? Are you reaching out beyond your cultural comfort zone? In other words, are there people around you who come from a cultural and/or ethnic background different from yours? Are you seeking to understand them better in order to reach them for Christ? If not, let me encourage you to do so. Not only will you experience the joy of obedience, but you also will begin to see the world through God's eyes.

The Nature of the Commission

That brings me to the nature of our commission. We have been called to a movement, the church. We have been commanded to make disciples of all of the nations—but the world we have been sent to is broken and confused. People desperately need the Lord.

Jesus did not want His disciples to miss that point. In fact, He gave them a challenge and a prayer request in Matthew 9:37–38 that speaks to the urgency of the need. He spoke of a plentiful harvest and the need to pray for workers for that harvest. However, in verse 36 Matthew allows us to look first into the heart of Jesus and see His motivation. Matthew says, "Seeing the people, He [Jesus] felt compassion for them, because they were distressed and dispirited like sheep without a shepherd."

What did Jesus see? He saw distressed, downcast human beings. He saw people who had no moral or spiritual direction ("sheep without a shepherd"), and it touched His heart. He was moved.

Compassion

I sometimes wonder if the truth of man's eternal separation from God has really sunk in with us. Oh, we believe it intellectually, but do we really believe it in our hearts? I mean, has the realization that Jesus Christ is the only way to God (John 14:6) and that to reject Him means an eternity in hell, become a part of us? The people we come in contact with can place their faith in Christ only during *this* life. There is no other opportunity. A genuine understanding of this will fill us with a sense of urgency, if not compassion.

Human beings apart from Jesus Christ and trapped in a crowded canyon of self-destruction with no hope are cause enough for compassion. Sin is one royal mess. It destroys families, shatters dreams, enslaves, gives a false sense of security, and is directly and indirectly the source of all our problems. Crime, wars, famines, oppression, injustice, disease, and a host of other maladies are the legacy of sin. All of us are affected. We are those who have sinned and those who have been sinned against. Sin spins a web that defies unraveling, and we are trapped in it. Psychologists, social engineers, governments and educators, and any number of society's other institutions may be able to offer temporary help, but only the Savior can give permanent help and, most important, eternal hope.

The Question

We have the answer. We can help people find that hope. The world is lost, and people need God's compassionate messengers. There never has been a time in history when the hearts of people have been more responsive than today. A loving, tender but clear presentation of the gospel, given in the power of the Holy Spirit, often will yield fruit. People are hungry for Christ. I have seen this to be true time and again, whether sharing the good news with a fellow passenger in an airplane or in a more formal public presentation.

The question is not whether non-Christians will respond to Christ. It is, Why aren't more Christians telling this wonderful news? God has prepared hearts, but so few seem willing to tell the message.

Jesus was moved to say, "The harvest is plentiful, but the workers are few. Therefore beseech the Lord of the harvest to send out workers into His harvest" (Matthew 9:37–38). Men and women whose hearts have been filled with compassion for those without Christ need to accept their role as part of God's movement. They need to commit themselves to the fulfillment of the Great Commission. They need to ask God to give them the boldness to tell the wonderful story of Jesus and His love.

Boldness is the product of the Holy Spirit. Fruitful witness is also the product of the Holy Spirit. Therefore, it is crucial to understand the relationship between our responsibility in helping to fulfill the Great Commission and the Power Source, the Holy Spirit. We will look at this in the next chapter.

9

THE POWER SOURCE

The Holy Spirit and the Great Commission

 od never intended for us to meet the greatest of all human needs—for people to know Christ—in our own strength. It is impossible to do.

Some of us have had to learn this the hard way. I have. I've had my share of failed, frustrated attempts at witnessing. Each time I am confronted with an opportunity to share my faith, I develop the proverbial knot in my throat, butterflies in my stomach, and often a twisted tongue. I'm nervous. I find this a bit unsettling to admit because I do this for a living—but it's true.

No matter how you slice it, telling others about Christ is an incredibly intimidating experience, and I admit also that I'm chicken—especially when I attempt to do God's work in the energy of the flesh.

A PROBLEM

Several years ago I was explaining the gospel to a young man. I made my way through the presentation and, although I sensed my nervousness, I thought it was one of my better presentations. I felt I had answered his questions and that he knew what he needed to do in order to trust Christ. I even had used my testimony to illustrate what Christ could do in a person's life. But as I walked away I had a gnawing feeling that something wasn't right. Something was missing. I mentally reviewed my approach and presentation and concluded that I had covered all the bases. So why the disturbing feeling? Then it hit me. Although the presentation was clear, I had been very "professional," and I had depended on the wrong person. I had trusted in myself and what I knew—and there was no power. I had not trusted God, through the power of the Holy Spirit, to use me as His instrument in this young man's life.

I have committed my life to help train and equip Christians to share their faith with others effectively. Training is crucial. However, too many of us depend more on our training, on evangelistic tools and events, and on strategies, than we do on God. Knowledge and strategy cannot produce fruit. That's the job of the Holy Spirit. This is the missing emphasis in much of today's evangelism. Someone once made the piercing observation that if the Holy Spirit were taken away from our Christian activity, we'd hardly know the difference. That may be somewhat overstated, but it does hit at whom and what we trust.

The fulfillment of the Great Commission is too big for any of us. The challenge is beyond our ability to perform, both in terms of our personal adequacy and the scope of the task. Only God can make it happen. Since we have been commanded to do it and only God can pull it off, then He has us where He wants us, totally dependent on Him. That actually is good news, because God never gives us a responsibility without also giving us the resources to carry it out.

The One who empowers us to accomplish the task is the Holy Spirit. There could be no salvation without the ministry of the Holy Spirit. He convinces men and women of their sinfulness and of their need for Christ (John 16:8). He causes a change in life, the new birth (John 3:5–6). He is the author of maturity in the Christian life (Galatians 5:22–25). He is the link between truth and transformation, between knowledge and action. Without obedient, active dependence on Him, we are doomed to mediocrity and failure in our witness for Christ.

WHO THE HOLY SPIRIT IS

Perhaps I'm getting ahead of myself. We need to answer two basic but very important questions. First, who is the Holy Spirit? Second, why did He come?

The Holy Spirit is the third person of the Trinity. As such, He is God, having all the attributes and personality of the godhead. The Holy Spirit is not inferior to the Father in any way. He is not simply some powerful angel, acting as some heavy-duty assistant to both God the Father and God the Son. He is not an impersonal "it," but a person. He has personality: the ability to think, feel, and act. This is difficult to understand, but the Bible clearly teaches it.

WHY THE HOLY SPIRIT CAME

Second, why did the Holy Spirit come? Many reasons could be given. Some are mentioned above. However, Jesus summarizes the purpose of the Holy Spirit's mission in the world in one crisp statement in John 16:14: "He [the Holy Spirit] will glorify Me, for He will take of Mine and will disclose it to you." The Holy Spirit came to glorify Christ. You can be sure that the Holy Spirit will never direct or lead us to do anything that would bring shame to Christ or be inconsistent with who He is. Quite the contrary. He has come to glorify Christ and to fulfill His mission for mankind. This is an important point to grasp. Unfortunately, some "Christians" have used the expression "the Holy Spirit led me" or similar language to justify selfish choices, if not outright sinful behavior. He leads and empowers us to obey God's Word.

If the Holy Spirit is God and He came to glorify Christ, that means God through the person and power of the Holy Spirit glorifies Christ through us. I realize that sounds simple, and it is. It also is a profound mystery. Somehow God uses the Holy Spirit, working through weak, powerless, and fallen human beings, to literally change the world. Jesus Christ has given us the Great Commission (to make disciples of all the nations); He has also given us the Resource (the Holy Spirit) to accomplish the task. Because we are weak, sinful creatures, we are totally inadequate for the assignment. Yet God, through the Holy Spirit, makes us adequate. *The willingness to obey, the ability to obey, and the fruit of obedience are the products of the Holy Spirit.* We will never be effective in evangelism until we recognize and submit to this principle.

THREE WAYS THE HOLY SPIRIT EMPOWERS

If this is true (and it is), then it is important to understand the role of the Holy Spirit in fulfilling the Great Commission through us. The Holy Spirit is involved in three empowering activities as they relate to evangelism and discipleship.

First, Jesus says in John 16:13, "When He, the Spirit of truth, comes, He will *guide you into all the truth*" (italics added).

His mission is to help us understand God's Word and to empower us to obey. He guides us into all the truth. This includes our understanding and recognition of our Lord's command to make disciples of all nations.

It is my conviction that any Christian who truly is filled with the Holy Spirit will have a desire to see men and women come to know Christ. He or she won't be able to help it. Since the Holy Spirit came to glorify Christ and to guide us into all truth, it is fair to conclude that He will glorify Christ by using us to introduce others to Him. The Holy Spirit gives us the desire and "burden" for those without Christ. That's why a prepared, yielded heart is the first step in effective evangelism. Simply attending an evangelism seminar or workshop will not make you a more fruitful witness for Christ. Granted, you'll be more knowledgeable, but we need supernatural assistance to be both obedient and fruitful. The Holy Spirit will only guide submissive Christians. If we are determined to do God's work in our strength, we can expect *our* results and not God's.

Sadly, it often takes failure and frustration before we give in. It's like the two year old who refused his father's help with tying his shoes. He protested, "I do it, I do it." The wise father stepped back and allowed his little boy "to do it." After several frustrating attempts, the little fellow submissively crawled into his father's lap and said, "Daddy help; Daddy help." That is exactly the role of the Holy Spirit, to help us by guiding us to fulfill God's commandment.

Second, not only does the Holy Spirit guide us into the truth about our part in the Great Commission, but He also gives us the power to fulfill it. After His resurrection, Jesus told His followers in Luke 24:49, "Behold, I am sending forth the promise of My Father upon you; but you are to stay in the city until you are clothed with power from on high." The expression "clothed" carries with it the idea of taking on the appearance of another.

My father has had a great influence on my life. I admire him more than any man in the world. When I was a child I loved to wear my father's clothes. I would try to walk like him, sit like him, and even talk like him. In almost every way I imitated him. I wanted to take on his appearance, bear his resemblance, be just like him.

As faithful followers of Christ, we bear the signature of the Holy Spirit, which is power. This power separates and distinguishes us from nonbelievers and disobedient Christians. Power is meant to be used, and we draw on this wonderful power source to overcome sin and temptation and to become imitators of Jesus Christ.

However, there is a more specific purpose for this power. Just before He returned to heaven, Jesus told His followers what was absolutely essential for them to be effective representatives of His cause. Acts 1:4 says, "Gathering them together, He commanded them not to leave Jerusalem, but to wait for what the Father had promised, 'Which,' He said, 'you heard of from me,'" and in verse 8, "'but you will receive power when the Holy Spirit has come upon you; and you *shall be My witnesses*'" (italics added).

Do you see the urgency and priority in these two verses? He commanded His followers not to leave Jerusalem but to wait there for the Holy Spirit to come into their lives. In other words, it would have been futile for them to even attempt to represent the interests of their Lord and Savior without the abiding presence of the Holy Spirit.

Wait before you act. That's an important principle. It's still an important principle for us to follow today. Although I understand verse 4 of Acts 2 to refer to the initial baptism of the Holy Spirit which inaugurated the church (now all Christians are baptized by the Holy Spirit at the time of salvation—1 Corinthians 12:13), the broader principle still applies. Before we seek to act on Christ's behalf, we must first be sure we are surrendered to the control of the Holy Spirit.

This is easier said than done. We live in a pragmatic environment. Doing has replaced being. In fact, a person's significance is often determined by what he or she accomplishes rather than by the depth and strength of the individual's character. In our pilgrimage of productivity and performance, we lose touch with our hearts and with the right motivation. We become powerless achievers and perhaps are recognized and applauded for our performance, but we are dismal failures in accomplishing anything of eternal significance. The only safeguard we have is to submit to the control and wait for the leading of the Holy Spirit. We should wait before we act.

In verse 8 Jesus told His followers what would happen as a result of their waiting for the Holy Spirit. "You will receive power . . . you shall be My witnesses." The specific purpose of the Holy Spirit's power is to produce witnesses. This, of course, is not the only way He works through our lives, but it is the primary demonstration of His power.

Those early followers of Christ made the message of the Cross the primary issue wherever they went. People knew about Him and His power to change lives. Government officials, poor people, the rich, even religious leaders—none could escape the loving but powerful gospel these empowered men and women presented. Both the message and the messengers were distinguished by the supernatural.

Their effectiveness in evangelism was not because they were outgoing, gregarious personalities. Some of us make the tragic error of communicating, either directly or indirectly, that only sharp, attractive people can be effective in initiative evangelism (where a person takes the initiative to share the gospel one-to-one). This is not true. The Holy Spirit is not held hostage to working through certain personality types. Bold witness is the result of the filling of the Holy Spirit (Acts 4:31). Every Christian who has the responsibility to tell about Christ, and we all do, also has the power available to do it.

If the criterion for effectiveness in evangelism is an outgoing personality, I'm in the wrong business. Really. I am naturally a somewhat private person. I don't like to intrude or pry into others' lives. I find this whole idea of witnessing somewhat intimidating. This may be your experience as well. However, I have discovered that I experience a supernatural boldness when I, by faith, choose to obey God and tell about Christ. This has happened time and again, despite my natural inclination, when I have submitted to the control of the Holy Spirit. This boldness to witness is a direct, specific result of the power of the Holy Spirit working through me.

The third way the Holy Spirit empowers us is by leading us to prepared hearts. One of the best examples of this principle is that of Philip the evangelist and his encounter with the Ethiopian eunuch (Acts 8:26–39). The story begins with the angel of the Lord instructing Philip to take a trip along the desert road from Jerusalem to Gaza (verse 26). As he rides along he comes upon this Ethiopian eunuch who is reading from the prophet Isaiah. At this point, Luke records, "Then the Spirit said to Philip, 'Go up and join this [Ethiopian] chariot'" (verse 29). In obedience, Philip does precisely as he is told. He explains to the Ethiopian what the Ethiopian has been reading (Isaiah 53:7–8) and its application to Jesus Christ. Having his understanding enlightened, the Ethiopian places his faith in Christ. With the mission accomplished, verse 39 says, "The Spirit of the Lord snatched Philip away."

Just as the Spirit of God led Philip to a prepared heart, so He leads us today. I don't mean to convey that His leading is necessarily in the same dramatic way as it was for Philip, but He does prompt us to share the gospel with certain people. In some cases the leading is obvious; in others it is not as apparent. In any event, we need to cultivate a sensitivity to the leadership of the Holy Spirit.

That's why it's so important to begin each day by asking God in prayer to lead you to those He wants you to talk to about Christ. Then expect God to do just that. It's amazing how many Spirit-led opportunities we can find to present the gospel when we expect them.

Does this mean we are to witness only when we sense we are being "led"? No. I believe we must pray and seek God's guidance, but we also should take the initiative—lovingly—in presenting the gospel to others. Look for the obvious point of need during the course of conversation with others, and then, if at all possible, address the need and turn the conversation to Christ. (For further information on sharing Christ effectively, I highly recommend two excellent books: *Witnessing Without Fear*, by Bill Bright, and *Tell It Often . . . Tell It Well*, by Mark

McCloskey.) It is just as futile to try to steer a parked car as it is to expect God to lead you without your taking a step of faith.

An incredible thing happened to me several years ago. I had a particular burden for the young men who attended a university in our city. I prayed for these students on a regular basis, asking God to bring them to a point of commitment to Christ. The more I prayed, the more I became convinced that God wanted to use *me* to share the gospel with them. I was impressed to witness personally to five of these young men. I set up individual appointments with them on the same afternoon. Then the miraculous happened. In less than three hours, all five of these men placed their faith in Jesus Christ!

TWO IMPORTANT LESSONS

I learned two very important lessons.

First, pay close attention to the individuals God gives you a concern for. It's the Spirit of God *speaking* to you.

Second, take advantage of that opportunity to share the gospel with them. It's the Spirit of God *leading* you.

That does not mean that every time you share the gospel that person will become a Christian. If he or she doesn't, does that mean we were *not* led by the Holy Spirit? Not necessarily. Sometimes the Holy Spirit will use us as "sowers," and other times we will be "reapers." Often He will use us as one link in a long chain of events which ultimately will bring a person to Christ. Our job is to obey. His job is to produce the fruit in His time.

It is impossible to fulfill the Great Commission without the empowering assistance of the Holy Spirit.

The Holy Spirit enables us to fulfill God's commandments.

The Holy Spirit gives us specific power to be His witnesses.

The Holy Spirit leads us to prepared hearts.

We must yield our lives to the power of the Holy Spirit if we want to live fruitful Christian lives, full of purpose. In the next chapter we'll look at how to do this.

10

UNDER HIS CONTROL

Living Fruitful and Purposeful Lives

ave you ever experienced "spiritual tiredness," a loss of joy and little or no energy to live the Christian life? Does it ever seem there is little progress in your spiritual development? Do you sometimes find yourself pressured to perform, outwardly conforming to rules and standards but with no inner sense of personal peace or freedom? Are you plagued by consistent failure and even sin in your life? Has the frustration of an up-and-down relationship with Christ caused you to settle for mediocrity? Do you sometimes feel spiritually trapped? Have you lost your desire for prayer, Bible study, and fellowship with other Christians? What about your view of God? Do you sometimes wonder whether or not He cares or if it is possible to please Him?

If you have experienced any of the above, this chapter is for you. Maybe I should say it more strongly. I believe every Christian, at one point or another, has wrestled with frustration and failure in the Christian life. If you haven't, you don't need this book. If you are like me, though, and have at times struggled and failed in your attempts to be a spiritually vibrant Christian, what I have to say in this chapter will be wonderful, liberating news.

As you saw in the previous chapter, God has given us His Holy Spirit so we can be more like His Son and so we can represent His business and priorities in the world. Unfortunately, most Christians do not draw upon this supernatural resource. The reason in some cases is old-fashioned, sinful disobedience. However, I am persuaded that most Christians don't experience

God's power moment by moment because they simply don't know how. Therefore, we continue to stumble through the Christian life making our own choices, determining our own direction, with no clear sense of purpose and little joy or power. Satan either does everything possible to hide this wonderful truth from God's people, or he causes so much confusion and distortion concerning the ministry of the Holy Spirit that we don't know what to believe. So, filled with fear and apprehension and, of course, not wanting to be labeled extremists, we continue, not only in our ignorance, but also in our powerless spiritual bondage.

What's the solution? *The filling of the Holy Spirit.* You might ask, *But what can I do to be filled with the Holy Spirit?*

I thought you would never ask.

THREE BASIC KINDS OF PEOPLE

In order to understand what it means specifically to be filled with the Holy Spirit, we need to take a look at the profile of the three basic kinds of people. In 1 Corinthians 2:12–3:3, the apostle Paul describes these three as "natural," "spiritual," and "men of flesh." The "natural man" is a non-Christian. He has no relationship with Christ and he cannot understand "the things of the Spirit of God" (2:14). Though he has little, if any, spiritual sensitivity, more often than not he will respect God's truth.

Then there is the "man of flesh," the carnal man. Unlike the natural man, this person is a Christian, but he is characterized by spiritual immaturity. However, 1 Corinthians 3:1–3 indicates there are two kinds of immature Christians. The first is what I call *innocently immature.* These are new Christians who simply have not had time to grow and mature in Christ. They are spiritual babies. Thus Paul writes: "And I, brethren, could not speak to you as to spiritual men, but as to men of flesh, as to infants in Christ. I gave you milk to drink, not solid food; *for you were not yet able to receive it*" (1 Corinthians 3:1–2, italics added). He does not condemn these Christians for their immaturity.

However, he does get a little tougher on the second kind of immature Christian, the *willfully carnal.* He pointedly says, "*Even now* you are not *yet* able, for you are *still* fleshly. For since there is jealousy and strife among you, are you not fleshly, and are you not walking like mere men?" (1 Corinthians 3:2b-3). Look at the time-related words: "even now," "yet," "still." Paul's point is that it's not a matter of information and adequate time. They've had both. It's a matter of disobedience. Carnal Christians refuse to act on or apply what they know. There is little outward distinction between a carnal Christian and a non-Christian. Paul asks, "Are you not walking like mere men?"

On the other hand, carnality can be difficult to detect. Knowledgeable Christians can be a dangerous lot. We often use our "theological" and "biblical" accuracy to camouflage our carnal hearts. We know all of the right answers. We can assess the issues critically from a Christian perspective. We are even able to justify sinful behavior by manipulating a few passages of Scripture.

There is one thing that carnal Christians have in common: self-reliance. Self is at the center of the carnal Christian's motivation. He has chosen to live the Christian life his way. He does not depend on the Holy Spirit—he depends on himself. The results include frustration, worry, guilt, legalism, a critical attitude, unbelief, and disobedience. No matter how hard he tries, he fails because self is at the center of his Christianity.

Obviously, God's desire is for all of us to be the third kind of Christian, the spiritual man. The spiritual person is the one who is directed and governed by the Spirit of God. He has supernatural insight and the ability to ascertain the will of God. His Christianity reflects pure motives and a deliberate reliance on the Holy Spirit (1 Corinthians 2:11-16).

Contrary to what some believe, being a spiritual Christian does not mean that a person has arrived at a point of sinless perfection. It does mean, however, that we are maintaining a constant and developing walk with Christ. We quickly respond in confession and repentance when the Holy Spirit points out sin and failure in our lives. This is what the Bible means by the expressions "Walk in the light as He Himself is in the light" (1 John 1:7); and, "Abide in Me, and I in you" (John 15:4). Each day we are becoming more like Christ (Romans 8:29).

The key to becoming a spiritual Christian is the filling of the Holy Spirit. What is the filling of the Holy Spirit? That question is prompted by Ephesians 5:18: "Do not get drunk with wine, for that is dissipation, but be filled with the Spirit."

To be filled with the Spirit means to be *controlled* by the Holy Spirit. It does not mean we receive the Holy Spirit—that took place when we trusted Christ as Savior and Lord (1 Corinthians 12:13). It does mean we are brought under His influence and control. We are aware of His presence and our need to be directed by Him. In the same way that wine alters and influences the behavior of one who is drunk, so in a more powerful way our behavior is influenced when we are filled with the Holy Spirit. It therefore means to give the Holy Spirit unhindered access to every area of our lives.

Some years ago when I began my speaking ministry, Karen and I often would stay in other people's homes. It didn't take us long to discover that there are basically two kinds of hosts. Some would subtly confine our movement in their home by politely hinting at what areas or rooms were "off limits." Then there were the many gracious hosts who would say "our house is your house. Make yourself at home." We knew that they meant it and we had complete freedom.

The Holy Spirit is not free to fill our lives because He is treated like a restricted guest, confined to the guest room, rather than being given the run of the house. The irony is that He owns the house. He actually deserves the freedom to go wherever He wants—and He wants unhindered access.

To be filled with the Spirit also means a character transformation. One who is filled with the Holy Spirit will evidence the fruit (character qualities) of the Spirit outlined in Galatians 5:22–23: "But the fruit of the Spirit is love, joy, peace, patience, kindness, goodness, faithfulness, gentleness, self-control." It is not my purpose to comment on each of these qualities, but I do think it is important to note that the word *fruit* is singular. It is not the "fruits of the Spirit" but the "fruit" of the Spirit. When one is filled with the Spirit, these character qualities are concurrently and simultaneously produced. Put another way, it is one fruit with nine manifestations. Notice too that it is the "fruit *of* the Spirit." The Holy Spirit produces the fruit naturally; it is not the product of human struggle or strain. Just as a properly nourished apple tree does not struggle to produce apples, one who is filled with the Holy Spirit does not struggle to produce the fruit of the Spirit. It just happens.

This is wonderful news. It gives all of us hope. Because of our consistent failure or rejection, or the damaging words of others, some of us have concluded we are who we are and we can never change. The fruit of the Spirit refutes this. The Holy Spirit specializes in enhancing and changing who we are. As we are brought under His control, He changes our hearts and attitudes; and in exchange He gives us these supernatural character qualities. He transforms our lives. God never intended for us to settle for failure or mediocrity in our Christian lives!

SPIRITUAL MATURITY

Here is a caution, though. If a person is filled with the Holy Spirit, he will evidence the fruit of the Spirit, but that fruit will not necessarily be mature or ripe. This speaks to the difference between spirituality and spiritual maturity. Everyone who is filled with the Spirit is spiritual, but not everyone who is filled with the Spirit is spiritually mature. The difference between the two is time and consistency. Spiritual maturity takes place when there is consistent application of truth over a period of time. Spirituality takes place the moment one is filled with the Holy Spirit. The person is spiritual in the sense that he is in touch with, or sensitized to, the things of the Spirit during the time he is filled with the Spirit. The consistent filling of the Spirit will accelerate the maturation process. In short, it is possible to be filled with the Spirit and not be spiritually mature, but it is not possible to be spiritually mature without being consistently filled with the Holy Spirit.

Some time ago Bob Boyd, a good friend of mine and an outstanding evangelist, shared this story with me over lunch:

A young Christian said to his pastor after discovering the filling of the Holy Spirit, "I really sense the power and filling of the Holy Spirit."

The pastor replied, "That's wonderful, but it's not difficult to fill a thimble. Pray that you will become a bucket."

That's the difference between spirituality and spiritual maturity.

OTHER RESULTS

Besides the fruit of the Spirit, Paul mentions four other results of the filling of the Spirit in Ephesians 5:19–6:4. They are thankfulness, communication, submissive spirits, and harmony in the home. In addition, when the Holy Spirit is in control, there is peace and joy; when we are in control, there is confusion and chaos. I can't think of any reason we wouldn't want to experience the supernatural benefits of the Spirit's control. Yet our stubborn, rebellious nature easily rejects and defies the notion of submission to anyone's authority but our own, even though in the case of the Holy Spirit it is for our own good and blessing. Even as Christians we can reject God's grace. That's what carnal Christians do.

To be filled with the Spirit is not just some good, optional advice. It is a command that leaves little room for interpretation and absolutely no room for bargaining or negotiation. The statement in Ephesians 5:18 is in the imperative mood, "Be filled with the Spirit." Again, God wants us to realize that this is not optional; it is vital in order to experience both power and purpose in the Christian life. If we are not filled with the Spirit, we are living in sinful disobedience. We cannot please God unless we are filled with the Holy Spirit.

A COMMAND FOR EVERYONE

In addition, since this is a command, and since the apostle Paul is addressing the church and not an individual, we must conclude that the command is for everyone. This may seem obvious. However, some Christians are under the erroneous impression that the filling of the Spirit is an experience reserved for those who they think are the Christian superstars. You know, people like Chuck Colson, Billy Graham, and Mother Teresa.

"After all," those Christians reason, "they are so well known, and they are doing such wonderful things for God." So they conclude they simply don't qualify for the same experiences the well-known Christians have.

That may be our conclusion, but that's not what the Bible teaches. Certainly God uses some people in unique, public ways.

That's undeniable. However, every Christian has been given the same command to be filled with the Holy Spirit and, therefore, has the same power source available to him to do the will of God. It's for everyone.

Also, the filling of the Spirit is a repeated experience. The expression "Be filled with the Spirit" is in the present tense. That implies continuous action. The filling of the Spirit is not a once-for-all action or experience. We are to be filled constantly with the Spirit. When we sin we have rejected the Holy Spirit's influence over our lives. His power has been broken and then we are no longer filled with the Holy Spirit.

I suppose, hypothetically, it would be possible to reach a point where we are permanently filled with the Spirit, but, because sin interrupts the Spirit's control, I don't know any living people who are at that point.

Sin is the issue here. Whenever we sin, we anger the Holy Spirit because we have chosen to go our own way. That's why Paul said in Ephesians 4:30, "Do not *grieve* the Holy Spirit of God (italics added)." The word *grieve* is a powerful word. It implies not only anger but also deep hurt because of great loss. In essence, the Holy Spirit is deeply wounded because we have rejected His loving, tender control of our lives. He is hurt. This is a moving look at God's pure motives toward us. God, through the Holy Spirit, wants to direct our lives—not to make us a bunch of miserable, lifeless clones, but to release His joy and power in us so we can be all He intended. That's why He does not violate our wills. He wants it to be our choice. When we sin, we must bring our lives back under the control of the Holy Spirit. God's method for doing this is found in 1 John 1:9: "If we confess our sins, He is faithful and righteous to forgive us our sins and to cleanse us from all unrighteousness." This verse does not speak to non-Christians, but to Christians who have not dealt with specific sins in their lives. The way to deal with sin is to confess it to God. The word *confess* literally means to "say the same thing" as God says about sin. It carries with it a deeper meaning than simply agreeing that what we said, did, or thought was wrong and sinful. Biblical confession also involves repentance, to turn away and forsake the sin because we are truly sorry for our disobedience.

Some of us only go through the motions of confession. We're not really sorry about what we have done. Our conscience bothers us enough for us to admit that what we did was wrong, but not enough to drive us to repentance.

It's like a young boy in a toy store who is tempted to steal a model airplane. He carefully looks around and concludes that no one is watching him. He quickly grabs the airplane and tucks it under his jacket. On the boy's way out of the store the security guard places a firm hand on his shoulder and asks, "Young man, what's that bulge under your jacket?"

The boy begins to cry and frantically pleads with the guard, "Sir, I'm sorry, so sorry. Please don't tell my parents."

The guard replies, "Son, I'm not so sure you are sorry for what you did. I think you're just sorry you got caught."

It's not that we can change ourselves, but our heart's attitude must be a sincere one, a commitment to turn away from the sin and rely on God through the Holy Spirit to help us overcome it.

A PROMISE

First John 1:9 also contains a wonderful promise. When we sincerely confess our sins, He promises to cleanse us and forgive us. He doesn't hold it against us, nor does He grant partial forgiveness. He forgives, and He cleanses us from "*all* unrighteousness." We must learn to accept His total forgiveness, and we must forgive ourselves. Perhaps you are haunted by sinful failure. You have confessed it to God and He has forgiven you, yet you don't feel forgiven. Are the guilt and pain still with you? Does hardly a day go by that you don't remind yourself of your failure? Has the self-imposed guilt robbed you of your freedom and joy? This does not need to be. On the basis of 1 John 1:9, God has forgiven our confessed sin. If you don't *feel* forgiven, recognize that God never lies and that by insisting on "staying unforgiven," you are disagreeing with what God has declared to be true. Believe Him, agree with His declaration that you are forgiven, and accept His forgiveness. If He has forgiven you, the issue is forever settled.

We are filled with the Holy Spirit by faith. It's not a matter of begging or pleading with God to fill us with His Spirit. He is not trying to tease us or hold out on us. He wants to give us, freely and lavishly, the power and joy that we need to live the Christian life. If we have met His requirement as outlined in 1 John 1:9, we can claim by faith the filling of the Holy Spirit.

If you are not sure at this very moment that you are filled with the Spirit, allow me to suggest that you pause and pray. Ask God to show you any sin in your life that you have not confessed to Him. List those sins that come to mind on a piece of paper. Don't force it, but be honest. Confess those *specific* sins to God and claim the promise of 1 John 1:9. In fact, I would suggest that you write "1 John 1:9" across the sheet of paper, and then destroy the paper. That's exactly what God has done to your sins. He has cleansed you, and He has destroyed your sins.

I would suggest that you also claim by faith, through prayer, the filling of God's Spirit. First John 5:14–15 says, "This is the confidence which we have before Him, that, if we ask anything according to His will, He hears us. And if we know that He hears us in whatever we ask, we know that we have the requests which we have asked from Him."

That is a wonderful promise. Since it is God's will that we be filled with the Spirit (Ephesians 5:18), we can see by this passage in 1 John that if we ask God in faith to fill us with His Spirit, He will do exactly that.

Because we are filled by faith, we should not depend upon our feelings. We may or may not feel anything. As long as we have met God's requirement outlined in 1 John 1:9, we can claim—by faith—God's promise to fill us. After all, our responsibility is to believe God's Word and obey—by faith. Emotions are deceptive, and they are subject to change. God's Word and His promised results are stable, sure, and changeless. Therefore, as we consistently are filled with the Holy Spirit, we will begin consistently to experience and demonstrate the fruit of that Spirit.

I want to stress again that sin interrupts the Spirit's control in our lives. Therefore, the *moment* we sin we must confess it to God and claim the fullness of the Holy Spirit.

The Holy Spirit's control is the cure for spiritual tiredness, legalism, frustration, or an up-and-down spiritual pilgrimage. He also frees us to appreciate our lives and personal significance from God's point of view. In fact, we'll take a look at this matter of significance in the next chapter.

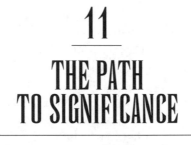

11

THE PATH
TO SIGNIFICANCE

Seeing God's Point of View

Walt Disney produced a movie entitled *The Incredible Journey*, a story about two dogs and a cat who went on a 250-mile trek through Canadian wilderness in search of their master. The film is full of adventure, chronicling the hair-raising experiences of these animals as they press toward their goal.

As members of the human race, we too are on an incredible journey. For many of us our pilgrimage is the search for significance. This quest has taken man through every conceivable experience; it has caused great frustration and sometimes even personal destruction for those who don't find significance, and it has brought great joy and fulfillment for those who do. You see, significance can be both elusive and intoxicating.

Webster's Third New International Dictionary defines significance as "the quality of being important; having consequence." For us, recognizing our significance is having a deep-seated understanding that "what I do and, more important, who I am really matter." I believe God created us with a longing to make our lives count (to be significant).

However, because of sin we have lost our perspective, and we continually look for significance in the wrong places. That's the reason disappointment and despair are so prevalent. The thinking goes, *If I can just find the right husband . . . now that I have this new job . . . if I can save enough money . . . if I can just get that house . . .*

The problem is that when we accomplish these things, we still have to answer the question, What difference does it make? You've heard about the guy who climbed the ladder of success and reached the top, only to discover the ladder was leaning against the wrong wall.

As I alluded to in an earlier chapter, there is nothing wrong with living in a nice house, having a rewarding career, and enjoying all the other fruits of your labor. I believe God wants us to enjoy life. We must remember, though, that the goal of life is not happiness—it is significance. True happiness comes as a *result* of a life of significance, a life based on what really matters.

Therefore, it is my purpose in this chapter to look briefly at the *source* of our significance and to identify *three biblical pillars* of significance. Understanding the issue from God's point of view is vital in recapturing and maintaining our sense of purpose.

THE SOURCE

The question is, What is the source of our significance? The apostle Paul gives us the answer in Galatians 2:20:

> I have been crucified with Christ; and it is no longer I who live, but Christ lives in me; and the life which I now live in the flesh I live by faith in the Son of God, who loved me and gave Himself up for me.

According to Paul, Jesus Christ gives our lives meaning and significance. When we allow Him to live His life through us, we bring significance to whatever we do and wherever we are. In this sense we also bring true happiness with us because we realize that the source of our significance is not in our occupation, our aspirations, or even in ourselves. Jesus Christ is the source of our significance. That's why Paul said in Philippians 1:21, "For to me, to live *is* Christ (italics added)."

In our competitive, rat-race culture, we Christians must fight to maintain this perspective. Everywhere we turn, the significant people in our lives—parents, peers, teachers, and most other "successful" role models—constantly define significance for us. If we are not careful and prayerful, we will become confused and begin to operate off everyone else's agenda rather than God's. The result is emotional stress, frustration, and a lack of inner peace. That's why many of us live our lives in a way that outwardly appears successful and significant, while inwardly we are haunted by the question, "Does my life really matter?"

Those of us who are involved in occupational Christian work are not immune to this significance syndrome. Unfortunately, we often take our eyes off the Lord and begin comparing our ministries with others. We sometimes privately wonder why we are not experiencing the same fruit, the same exposure, and the same recognition that some of our peers seem to enjoy. This is a dangerous position to be in. Our motivation for service becomes competition and dominance rather than wholeheartedly doing the will of God and leaving the results with Him. Or we lose our hope and confidence; discouragement sets in, and we wonder, *Is what we have done for Christ significant?*

The cure is to lift our sights and fix our gaze on Jesus Christ. Remember, we are crucified with Christ. We have nothing to prove but our loyalty and faithfulness to Him and to His will for our lives. When that is our commitment, we can be sure that what we do is eternally significant!

As Christians, how do we maintain the right perspective on this critical issue of significance? As we look at the three biblical pillars, we will see that, combined, they can form our overall perspective on significance.

First Biblical Pillar

The first is:

You cannot fully determine the significance of your life when you evaluate it at any given point in life.

When we become consumed and preoccupied with analyzing our significance, more often than not, distortion is the result. Time is the acid test. I am persuaded that God does not allow us to see the full impact of our lives because we simply couldn't handle it. The jury is still out.

More than 150 years ago, reports of an entertainer named

Tom Thumb hit the front pages of London newspapers. He and his variety show had performed before the royal court. He received rave reviews. Somewhere in the back of those same newspapers a brief paragraph appeared about a little-known scientist who had just written a book. The name of the book was *The Origin of Species*. The author: Charles Darwin.

Tom Thumb did not leave a lasting impact on the fabric of society, except for our entertainment. On the other hand, almost everyone has experienced the impact of Darwin's theory of evolution.

In that great chapter of faith, Hebrews 11, the writer specifically speaks to the issue of prematurely evaluating the significance of our lives. There are three types of faith outlined in the chapter: (1) victorious faith; (2) enduring faith; and (3) legacy faith. However, many messages on this passage tend to focus only on victorious faith. To be sure, the result of exercising our faith is *ultimate* victory, but there are times when God does not want us to experience physical healing, deliverance, or favorable response to our prayer requests for promotion, position, or possessions. God says no in order to keep us focused on His glory and His purposes. If He never told us no, or wait, He would be held hostage to our desires, and our source of significance would be lodged in what He does for us rather than in who He is and what He wants to do in and through us.

That's why the writer of Hebrews wants us to appreciate the enduring and legacy qualities of faith. After chronicling those who *did* experience miraculous victories because of their faith, he introduces us to those who endured and who exercised faith for the generations to come (legacy). Look closely at Hebrews 11:35b–40.

> Others were tortured, not accepting their release, so that they might obtain a better resurrection; and others experienced mockings and scourgings, yes, also chains and imprisonment. They were stoned, they were sawn in two, they were tempted, they were put to death with the sword; they went about in sheepskins, in goatskins, being destitute, afflicted, ill-treated (men of whom the world was not worthy), wandering in deserts and mountains and caves and holes in the ground. And all these, having gained

approval through their faith, did not receive what was promised, because God had provided something better for us, so that apart from us they would not be made perfect.

These men and women are the ones God underscores as being significant. Let's face it, the world would call all these people losers. Suffering and misfortune seemed to dominate their lives. They didn't qualify for the "beautiful people set." They could hardly be called winners. They weren't part of the establishment. They simply believed God and paid a dear price as a result.

Yet God said they were "men of whom the world was not worthy," those who "gained approval through their faith." They had the faith to endure because they realized their importance and significance was not tied to this life or the approval of others. The only thing that mattered was God's approval. That meant more to them than even life itself.

Was their faith in vain? Absolutely not! True, they did not experience what they were believing God for in their lifetimes. God wanted their lives to serve both as monuments of encouragement and as spiritual seeds that would bear incredible fruit in the generations to come. That's why the writer says in verse 40, "God had provided something better for us, so that apart from us they would not be made perfect." We are the living legacy of what they suffered and died for. We are enjoying the blessings and fruit of their faith. I am so glad they didn't give up or compromise. I wonder, *Where would we be if they had looked to their accomplishments as their source of significance?* That's a frightening thought.

I have enjoyed a fruitful ministry. I am convinced it is due in part to my great-grandfather Peter. Peter was a former slave who, I am told, was committed to a life of prayer. He didn't have much of this world's goods, and he obviously was denied the rights and privileges that I enjoy—but he prayed. Admittedly, I don't know what he prayed for, but I do know that he did not experience in his lifetime the fulfillment of his hopes and dreams.

When I speak to large audiences, board an airplane, or sit in a meeting, I am often reminded of Peter Loritts. His memory helps to keep me humble, and it reminds me that I am part of the legacy of his prayer life. I stand on his shoulders.

Peter is buried in the cemetery next to a small Methodist church in Conover, North Carolina. According to the world's standards, he was an obscure former slave who never accomplished anything of great significance. God says, "Not so!"

You see, you cannot fully determine the significance of your life when you evaluate it at any given point in life.

Second Biblical Pillar

The significance of your life is not determined by what you do.

The book of 1 Corinthians was written because the church at Corinth was afflicted with a distorted sense of self-importance. The church had deteriorated into cliques and factions. The people allowed their pride to get out of hand. There were three primary "clubs" in the church: (1) those who followed Peter; (2) those who followed the silver-throated orator Apollos; and (3) those who followed Paul. It wasn't loyalty that got the church into trouble—it was pride. The jockeying for position, recognition, and dominance divided the church. Obviously those great spiritual leaders (Peter, Apollos, and Paul) did nothing to encourage this sinful behavior. They simply became innocent objects through whom the people could justify their seemingly insatiable hunger for significance.

Paul, desiring to put an end to this madness, wrote a direct letter to the church, outlining his specific concerns and trying to get them to adjust their perspective.

In 1 Corinthians 4:1–5 he tells the Corinthians what he wants them to say about him. The applicational message of this passage is that our sense of significance and self-worth should not come from our position or occupation, no matter how noble it may be.

In verses 1 and 2 Paul states his perspective on his job: He is a servant of Christ and a steward of "the mysteries of God," and as such he makes it clear that his primary responsibility is to "be found trustworthy."

Paul reminds us that our primary calling is to Christ. He

says he is a servant of Christ; he is directed by Christ; he lives for Christ; he is available and willing to do whatever his Lord wants him to do. Jesus Christ is first and foremost. Too many Christians have become servants to jobs, professions, or possessions. If we allow that to happen, those things own us. We get our identity and significance from them and feel we are nothing without them. Yet nothing—and no one—should own us but Christ.

Next, Paul says he is a steward of the mysteries of God. The church is called a mystery in the Scriptures, so the expression "mysteries of God" refers to Paul's occupation as an apostle to the church. The word *steward* has to do with his approach to his position. *Steward* comes from the Greek word *oikonomia* (we get the English word *economy* from this Greek word). The idea is managing that which belongs to another. Paul did not have a proprietor attachment to his ministry. It was God's ministry, and he was called to execute and manage what God placed in his charge.

Just as nothing and no one should own us but Christ, so we also must accept the reality that we own nothing. God has simply given us the responsibility of taking care of His property and His opportunities that come our way until He comes. The problem with many of us is that we have a proprietor's attachment to our ministries and other responsibilities. When we lose our jobs, our egos are devastated because it was "my" job and "my" significance that were lost with the position.

This may very well be part of the problem many men experience during the "midlife crisis." For years these men have taken ownership of that over which they have no ultimate control. Intertwined with that ownership is their sense of fulfillment, significance, and happiness. When the inevitable takes place—personal failure, unfulfilled expectations, or the unpredictable nature of life—it's time for a major reevaluation. Some have a crisis. For others, however, this can be a constructive time, a time for soul-searching and spiritual inventory, a time for recommitment and dedication to Christ's ownership, a time to give their failures and unfulfilled dreams to Him in exchange for His unconditional love and acceptance.

Paul stresses that his primary responsibility as a steward is to be found trustworthy. If we are possessed by Christ and managers (stewards) of what belongs to Him, we are held accountable for the faithful execution of that calling. We must prove ourselves to be worthy of His trust. Notice the focus. Nowhere in this text does Paul point to the acceptance and approval of others as his criteria for significance. His one and only criterion is what God thinks. Paul realized that life was both too short and too precious to succumb to any other motivation.

Three Principles

Paul strongly desired his readers to see him in this light and adopt the same perspective. In fact, in verses 3 through 5 of 1 Corinthians 4, this perspective is bolstered by three overriding principles. First, *no "human court" has the authority to determine your significance* (verse 3). Paul is not saying we should not be accountable to other Christians and those in positions of spiritual leadership for our growth and development in Christ. It is sinful not to be accountable. His point is that our calling and significance are not in the hands of human beings. They are determined solely by God.

Second, *do not take yourself too seriously* (verse 4). Paul says, "I am conscious of nothing against myself." This must be taken to mean that Paul was not preoccupied with self-examination or self-importance. The key word is *conscious*. Our problem is that we are often too conscious about ourselves. We are aware of how significant and important our "moves" are. We need to be reminded daily that the role of a servant is to represent and meet the needs of the one he serves. In so doing he discovers his significance.

Third, *let God be the judge* (verses 4 and 5).

> The one who examines me is the Lord. Therefore do not go on passing judgment before the time, but wait until the Lord comes who will both bring to light the things hidden in the darkness and disclose the motives of men's hearts; and then each man's praise will come to him from God.

Spiritual Vision

As Christians, we should make sure these three concepts—servanthood, stewardship, and trustworthiness—form the core of our outlook on our jobs and other responsibilities. It's dangerous to ignore these things and try to do God's job. You can't. Too many of us are trying to determine whose life is "significant," which ministry is "significant," or what church is really doing "significant" ministry.

The truth of the matter is, we don't know and we don't see things the way God does. When we stand before Him, He will pass out the rewards, and I suspect we will be surprised at the outcome. I am reminded of what Jesus said to Peter when Peter was apparently concerned that John would be given a more "significant" opportunity. Jesus said, "What is that to you? You follow Me!" (John 21:22). In essence Jesus told Peter to mind his own business. The Christian community could use a good dose of that advice these days.

Third Biblical Pillar

That brings me to the third and final aspect of finding significance:

The significance of our lives is determined by our obedience.

Shortly before his death Joshua, the great warrior, gathered the Israelites together in the valley of Shechem. He reminded them of God's great blessing on them throughout their history. He recounted their miraculous victories and God's supernatural intervention on their behalf. They had tasted significance from God's point of view. However, Joshua realized that if his people were to continue to experience this significance, they had to make a choice.

He challenged them:

Now, therefore, fear the Lord and serve Him in sincerity and truth; and put away the gods which your fathers served beyond the River and in Egypt, and serve the Lord. And if it is disagreeable in your sight to serve the Lord, choose for yourselves today whom you will serve: whether the gods which your fathers served which were beyond the River, or the gods of the Amorites

in whose land you are living; but as for me and my house, we will
serve the Lord. (Joshua 24:14–15)

Joshua told the people that the significance of their lives
was in their hands. If they obeyed God and served God, the
result would be blessing (significance). If they turned to the idols
and pressures of a godless culture, they would become what they
served, something with a life of no consequence. He reminded
them that no one could make the decision for them: "Choose for
yourselves today whom you will serve." However, his resolve
was unshakable: "As for me and my house, we will serve the
Lord."

Though thousands of years separate us, the issue is still the
same: Where are we going to go to find our significance?
Beyond the "River" and in "Egypt"? Or to the unfailing, faithful
Lord of history? We too must decide whom we will serve. The
process can be difficult and painful, but the issue is simple. Significance is a choice. The choice is the object of our obedience.

Bill Klem was a major league baseball umpire who was
widely respected. He was a massive man weighing in excess of
three hundred pounds. Whenever he was behind the plate calling
the game, he maintained control. In fact, few had the courage to
challenge his calls.

However, in one game things did get a bit out of hand. It
was a classic situation: the bottom half of the ninth inning, and
the score is tied. Two outs and a runner on third base. The pitch-
er hangs a curve ball over the plate. The batter hits a shallow
single just over the third baseman's head. The left-fielder races
toward the ball, picks it up with his bare hand, and makes a perfect one-bounce throw to home plate. Problem: The ball and the
third base runner arrive at home at the same time. There is a col-
lision, and a cloud of dust explodes at home plate. In the confusion, both teams forget who's calling the game and they race out
of the dugout and off the field screaming repeatedly, "He's safe!"
"He's out!"

In the midst of the confusion, Bill Klem throws off his
umpire's mask, holds up his two massive arms, and shouts, "He
ain't nothin' until I call it!"

In a very real sense, the significance of our lives depends

on us. It's our call. It's in our hands. We can choose to obey God, or we can choose to chase the elusive, empty promises and processes the world deems as giving significance—but *we* have to make the choice. No one can decide for us. Just as Joshua couldn't do it for the Israelites, so no one can do it for us.

There is not an issue in life in which we cannot choose God's way, and when we obey Him, the results are eternal.

12

A PLEA FOR PERSPECTIVE

Five Principles for Maintaining a Sense of Purpose

 friend said to me years ago, "Crawford, if you have a good *why* for living, you can stand almost any *how*."

I have not forgotten that. If we have the right purpose (the "why"), it will give stability to our lives, anchor us during those inevitable hard times, and edit our priorities. If we build our lives on the wrong purpose, we can expect to experience aimlessness, confusion, and ultimate emptiness.

I have written this book because I am deeply troubled by the subtle but devastating influence of the combined forces of apathy, materialism, and self-centeredness upon Christianity in the American culture. We are, in effect, redefining God's purposes to meet our needs. Think of it. We presume to edit God rather than adjust our lives to His standard!

INFLUENCING OUR CULTURE

Although our churches are full, we are having comparatively little impact on our culture. As you read these words today, drugs and drug-related violence have reached epidemic proportions. Washington, D.C., is the murder capital of the country. It is predicted that within a few years not a family in this country will have escaped the awesome, vicious impact of AIDS. Socially and economically, we have created a permanent underclass who are trapped in America's basement, filled with hopelessness and despair. Abortion, legalized murder of unborn children, has become an acceptable form of birth control, performed by unscrupulous, greedy doctors, in many cases upon confused and frightened young women. Marriages are breaking up because couples are no longer "happy" with each other, or they have found someone else, or their present partner is a liability to their future success, or they have "irreconcilable differences."

I could go on, but you get the picture. I firmly believe God is setting the stage now for one of the greatest spiritual awakenings this country has ever experienced—but He is waiting for us. He wants His people to make the choice to live out that which we have been given in Christ, a life of purpose.

It's one thing to have something, and it's quite another to use it. The purpose of an automobile is transportation. If you own one but don't use it, it's silly to complain about not being able to get around.

God has given to the Christian community what the world needs—purpose. Ironically, many of us have become like the world and as a result have drifted away from our purpose. We send confusing signals. For example, even those of us who are involved in "Christian social activism" must be careful that our causes don't obscure the ultimate purpose, Jesus Christ. The cause is to be the vehicle to carry the message.

Sometimes we do not distinguish between hatred for sin and a judgmental attitude. We don't always distinguish between a person's sin and his need to know the Savior. We are known more for our denunciation of evil than for our hearts of compassion. We see little weeping for the lost condition of men and women, but a lot of lobbying for position and prominence.

MAINTAINING OUR SENSE OF PURPOSE

God has called us to express our commitment to Christ through many different professions and platforms. He has designed it this way so we can permeate society with the message of Christ. This is our purpose, and it must become our passionate commitment.

Our challenge is maintaining this perspective without succumbing to compromise. Paul had this very concern for his dear young friend, Timothy. Paul's advice to Timothy sums up what I have attempted to say in this book. He said in 2 Timothy 4:1–5:

> I solemnly charge you in the presence of God and of Christ Jesus, who is to judge the living and the dead, and by His appearing and His kingdom: preach the word; be ready in season and out of season; reprove, rebuke, exhort, with great patience and instruction. For the time will come when they will not endure sound doctrine; but wanting to have their ears tickled, they will accumulate for themselves teachers in accordance to their own desires, and will turn away their ears from the truth and will turn aside to myths. *But you, be sober in all things, endure hardship, do the work of an evangelist, fulfill your ministry.* (italics added)

This last sentence is the crux of the matter. Paul summarizes for his young friend what he must do to maintain his sense of purpose while living and ministering in a culture hostile to Christianity. The sentence contains five important principles.

Concentrate on Your Uniqueness

This principle is summed up in the opening two words of the sentence, "But you . . ." In the preceding verses Paul had described the condition of the society Timothy faces, the pressures and the uphill battle of ministry, and the rejection he will have to experience. Clearly Paul wanted Timothy to know, in the words of Elisabeth Elliot, that Jesus Christ did not call us to a playground but to a battlefield.

During our bleak, dark days, the focus should not be on what's happening to us or on what is going on around us. Rather, our clear concentration must be on our relationship with God and what He wants us to do in any given situation or circumstance. We must not allow the pressures of life to dictate our response. God through His Word and His Spirit will lead us.

This will cause us to operate from a position of strength and not from reaction. When we hit a "brick wall" or we become confused about direction, the first question we should ask is, "What does God want me to do?"

Again, the focus is not on what's going on out there, but on your relationship with God. As that relationship with Him is nurtured and developed consistently, He will give you your unique, tailor-made response and direction.

Be Aware of Your Environment

"Be sober in all things." The word *sober* has to do with a conscious awareness of what's going on. It is the idea of understanding the tapestry of your culture. John Stott, the great British preacher, observes that Christian leaders throughout history who made a difference for Christ and His cause had a firm handle on two things. First, they were students of their contemporary culture. They were familiar with the great issues of their day and the needs of the people. Second, those men and women were immersed in the Scriptures. Because of these two things, they were able to bridge the gap between human need and God's solution. Therefore, they were able to give a powerful, appropriate word from God for their culture.

It's amazing how uninformed many Christians are. Too many of us tend to be unprepared, lazy thinkers who have a one-dimensional perspective on the issues. We do very little reading or discussion of issues that are not strictly "Christian." That's precisely why, by the time we do respond, we are typically ten or fifteen years behind the times, answering questions that nobody is asking any longer. We need God's perspective and His creative solutions for the problems of the homeless, pornography, AIDS, the drug epidemic, greed and materialism, racism, etc.

On the other hand, some Christians want to have a prophetic role in our culture but give us only one political perspective. Righteousness and justice are not to be imprisoned by political structure. Our role is to lovingly hold all accountable to God's truth. If you are going to pick up the mantle of a prophet, you must realize that prophets historically have not been very popular people. In fact, they were often considered noisy nuisances, reminding everybody of God's perspective and His Word. Unless our present-day "prophets" are willing to pay this price, I would suggest they have the spiritual and intellectual integrity to lay the mantle down.

The word *sober* also implies the idea of the urgency of life.

We only have one life. A friend of mine, Blaire Cooke, often challenges Christians with this statement: "Life is but a brief moment in history lodged between two vast eternities. What are you going to do with your moment?"

That's the question, isn't it? To be sober means to concentrate on your moment. We will never pass this way again. Therefore, we have to pour our God-given purpose into that moment.

Expect to Suffer

"Endure hardship." This perhaps is the most difficult pill of all to swallow. None of us wants to go through hard times. God provides us with good times, times in which we prosper and experience relative calm. We should enjoy those times, but as you well know, they don't last forever.

As I have suggested in this book, suffering and hard times are woven into the tapestry of life. It's God's process of refinement and personal development. Hardship drives us to our knees and teaches us how to depend upon God to meet our needs and to sustain us. For those who endure, the resolve and commitment to follow Christ and fulfill His purposes have been strengthened. Endurance is the necessary stuff of character. It authenticates our message. We are visible testimonies of God's power and grace, and we become a source of encouragement and blessing to others.

The key word is *endure*. I enjoy watching distance runners. Their sleek, trim bodies are driven by a sense of timing and endurance. Their skill in running distances has been painfully refined through discipline and pushing themselves to endure sore muscles and lungs that feel as if they will explode at any moment. Day after day these athletes run to improve their time and build their endurance. They realize that the day of the race is too late to prepare. The race is the test of their endurance. The race proves whether or not they have the stuff to win. That's why they endure the hardship beforehand.

You may be extremely talented. God may have given you abilities and gifts that can be of great service to His cause. You want the opportunity to use them, but perhaps you are like an incredibly gifted man I know. When the pressures come he "runs." Then he wonders why his ministry is not having a broader impact.

One day I said to him, "God won't give you the platform you think you deserve because you won't stick around. You won't be there long enough for Him to develop in you the character you need to handle the opportunity."

Hardship is God's tool to make us useful instruments, so don't run from it. Stay there. Endure hardness.

Focus on the Core of the Cause, the Cross

"Do the work of an evangelist." Timothy probably was not a gifted evangelist. There is abundant evidence from both 1 and 2 Timothy that he was a gifted pastor-teacher. Yet, in so many words, Paul reminds his young friend not to forget the core of this thing called Christianity, the cross of Jesus Christ. Paul wanted Timothy to make sure that, along with his other important activities, he was involved in introducing men and women to the Savior. This was to be an essential pillar of his ministry.

It is popular today in some Christian circles to become armchair analysts and theorists. Some of us can articulate masterfully what's wrong with the world, but when it comes time to share the solution, Jesus Christ, we are tongue-tied. Certainly we must be comprehensive in our Christianity and minister to the felt needs of people, including ministering to Christians who are developing in their relationship with Christ. Yet we must never get so complicated or "sophisticated" in our Christianity that the call to the Cross is abandoned. If we do, as far as God is concerned, we have no message.

James Denny, the famed nineteenth-century Scottish preacher, said, "The simplest truth of the gospel and the profoundest truth of theology must be put in the same words: He bore our sins."

Pursue Faithfulness and Obedience

"Fulfill your ministry." It is important to look at the order of these three words. Paul did not tell Timothy to "draw fulfillment from your ministry." Personal fulfillment is not the issue.

The call of God (His will for our lives) is *objective*. Thus, our personal happiness and fulfillment is not the primary issue. The emphasis is on fulfilling the task, completing the assignment.

One of our greatest American preachers, Phillips Brooks, said, "Oh, do not pray for easy lives; pray to be stronger men and women. Do not pray for tasks equal to your powers; pray for powers equal to your tasks. Then the doing of your work will be no miracle, but you shall be the miracle."

In verses 6 through 8 Paul gives a word of personal testimony as an example of these five principles and a life full of purpose. He opens his heart to his young friend Timothy. Paul's life is coming to an end and, in essence, he gives his own eulogy. He reminds Timothy that he has poured his life out for others. He has sought to be a model, an example. He has no regrets. In verse 7 he says, "I have fought the good fight, I have finished the course, I have kept the faith." He completed the assignment.

Paul realized he might die in obscurity with little or no recognition in the eyes of the world, but he had come to terms with that issue long ago. He knew that God cared, and that nothing went beyond His scrutiny. That's why Paul could say in verse 8, "In the future there is laid up for me the crown of righteousness, which the Lord, the righteous judge, will award to me on that day; and not only to me, but also to all who have loved His appearing."

He was a man of passionate commitment. He lived a life of purpose.

And you can, too!

A PASSIONATE COMMITMENT

STUDY GUIDE

he whole idea of a passionate commitment to God implies action. Without the application of these truths, true discipleship is not possible. Many books encourage us to fulfill our high purpose in Christ, yet leave us to figure out how to follow through on their principles. This author continues to call for a wholehearted response—a doing rather than mere believing. This study guide is intended to supplement this call to action by giving additional ways of living out our faith as well as sharing it with others. It is my hope that if you are moved by this excellent message, you will follow through with these exercises based on the book and be able to measure concrete growth in your commitment to Christ.

James S. Bell, Jr.

CHAPTER 1

GETTING THE
MOST OUT OF LIFE

1. Darryl did not deliberately choose to be a lukewarm Christian or commit serious sin. What were the major causes of his spiritual dryness? Why do you think he was not aware of the reasons for his lack of joy or enthusiasm?

2. Darryl's life was consumed with worthy goals and activities. Yet those "demands of the present" inhibited his spending time with his family and God. Examine your own activities apart from God and family. How might they be absorbing too much of your time and energy?

3. List all the spiritual activities you performed on a regular basis over the last year. Which ones bore fruit in your own life and the lives of others? What are the main reasons that these disciplines met expectations and produced positive results?

4. Which spiritual duties have left you cold or relatively unfulfilled in the last year? Why do you think you may have failed to please God in these particular duties? What elements have changed from previous periods when they had more meaning and effectiveness?

5. The author mentions a gospel of self-indulgence and personal prosperity as being invalid. Even if you do not personally confess a belief in this message, perhaps it has crept into your spiritual walk in subtle ways. Where has your own well-being or pleasure superseded the demands of the Christian life?

CHAPTER 2

MAKING
WISE CHOICES

1. How have apathy and materialism influenced your choices? What decisions have you made lately that reflect your eternal perspective on life? In what ways has advancing human wisdom actually contributed to our problems? What does God say in His Word about human wisdom?

2. None of us is exempt from the pains and pressures of life. If we tie up our worth in what we have or what we can achieve, both God and circumstances can humble us. Recall a disappointment or tragedy in which your limitations and powerlessness became apparent. How did you learn to depend on God and gain His perspective?

3. What adverse circumstances in the past have tempted you to make material possessions the solution? In what ways has the ownership of more things actually made you discontent and kept you farther away from God? What false promises or security do certain things hold in your life and later fail to deliver?

4. Everything we have comes from God. Make a list of the more obvious gifts and blessings that you may thank God for on a regular basis. Now make a second column of the more subtle yet major blessings (such as the ability to walk and talk) that you often take for granted. Try to thank God in prayer for three different gifts each day over the next week.

5. All that we do should be valued in the light of eternity. When have you had to sacrifice short-term temporal gains in light of eternal values and rewards? Conversely, identify a situation when you chose earthly gains over eternal benefits. What decisions do you now face in which these two choices will compete, and how will you decide?

CHAPTER 3
NEW TESTAMENT DISCIPLESHIP

1. Though we need to guard against the godless influence of the world, we need to be instruments of God's love in the world. Explain in your own words the two extreme positions of avoiding the world altogether or conforming to its behavior. In your own life situation, how can you be *in* the world but not *of* it? What fears or issues are barriers to your full commitment to the discipleship process?

2. Define in your own words what it means to be discipled. What truths in Scripture have you best put into practice beyond merely believing? What would you say are the most difficult truths or teachings for you to obey? Is there someone you know who models the life of Christ? Seek to learn from and imitate his or her behavior.

3. It is important to be "verbally correct" in our confession of faith, yet this may substitute for correct actions. Analyze areas in your Christian walk where mere verbal commitment was not followed up with leaving your comfort zone and living out the full implications of our faith. Find one command of Christ in Scripture that you have a difficult time obeying, and seek the Lord for grace.

4. The procrastinating disciple has great intentions but delays carrying out the commands of Christ. Take a look at your holy resolutions over the past year. What impeded your progress (both internally and externally)? Consider one important task for Christ that you are putting off and do it now.

5. The undecided disciple can't make up his or her mind whether to follow through, especially with difficult acts of obedience. The author mentions self-interest, unbelief, and distraction. Write a summary of how these obstacles hinder firm commitment. Pray about other root causes for indecision that leads to sin.

CHAPTER 4
PAYING
THE PRICE

1. What is the focus of your love? Do you love our Lord more than Christian activity, your church, or even your family? If a choice has to be made, are you willing to identify with Christ and His sufferings even at the risk of losing the acceptance of your peers and those you count as significant?

2. Are there distractions and encumbrances that hinder your availability to God? What are they? Are you willing to part with them immediately if necessary? How might you simplify your life in order to love God more?

3. The message of the Cross may be offensive to some because it includes repentance and self-denial. It undercuts the vanity and pride of the world. First, are you living the message of the Cross in order to legitimately proclaim it? Second, are you then sharing that message unashamedly regardless of the personal cost to you? How might you better bring these two directives together?

4. Be honest with yourself about your attitude toward the things you own. Do you seek to control their use? Is there any worry, greed, pride, or consumption tied to them? Do you see yourself as a steward or an owner? Are you afraid to surrender all to God to use or withdraw as He sees fit? Acknowledge Him the owner of all you possess right now.

5. Excessive debt and other worldly commitments can prevent you from becoming available to God when needed. Because the debtor is a slave to the lender, you "mortgage" your future time for God. Scan the areas in your life where you may have taken on a worldly master—finances, other people, hobbies, career, etc. Turn these over to God in order to become available to serve Him.

CHAPTER 5

THE CRITICAL DECISION

1. Have you made the critical decision of surrendering all that you are to Christ? What about your thought life? Is your mind being transformed through the consistent, disciplined study of God's Word? Do you have any goals for Bible study? Why not establish a few?

2. Read through the first eleven chapters of Romans in order to understand the background as to why you are able to present your body as a holy sacrifice acceptable to God. Summarize (1) what it means to be lost; (2) Jesus Christ as the solution; (3) the Spirit-filled life overcoming sin and temptation; and (4) our spiritual heritage in Christ. How do these points help you better understand your ability to do the will of God?

3. Is your lifestyle in any way influenced by the expectations of the world? Are you living a "split personality" existence where some choices are determined by God's Word and others by worldly standards or the approval of others? Declare your full allegiance to God's standard in all ventures and seek His help to reveal the deepest attitudes of your heart.

4. Take a careful inventory of how you feed your mind. Begin by looking at the last month—books, newspapers, magazines, TV, film, music. Make columns with three categories—negative, neutral, positive. How did the negative elements hurt your spiritual walk or even neutralize the positive input? On the other hand, how did Bible study or other Christian input transform your worldview and help prevent your falling into wrong thinking and sin?

5. To be a disciple ultimately means to be disciplined. What key qualities (such as faithfulness and self-control) are needed for the disciplined life? After you've listed at least six, apply them to all the key functions in your life. What are your chief strong and weak points? How can God's grace help you to strengthen your weak spots?

CHAPTER 6

PURSUING A LIFE OF PURPOSE

1. How do you usually make decisions concerning life's choices and direction? What decisions are you facing in which you need to determine God's will? In what ways has God reminded you of your need to operate from His agenda and not yours?

2. One sign of the importance of our discipleship is the eternal destiny of the souls of those around us. Make a list of at least three persons that you will commit to pray for in terms of their salvation on a regular basis. Make a commitment to share your faith with at least one person if God opens a way.

3. Discerning the will of God is, of course, critical to obeying His purposes for your life. Examine the five criteria listed in this chapter to discover God's will related to a particular decision. Consider one important decision you need to make in the near future in which you need God's clear direction. Go through the process carefully and then make the decision based on the results. How much did this process aid you in making a better decision from His perspective?

4. To "walk in a worthy manner" before God is the product of what we allow Him to first do in us. Take one specific command in Scripture and begin by praying for the Lord to give you insight into its meaning and grace to carry it out. Then begin to write out ways in which you might obey this precept. Finally, go out and perform this task with all your heart and soul.

5. Recall the times in your life when you knew you couldn't make it without God's intervention. Did He come through? How did He manifest His power? As you consider becoming a more committed disciple, compile a list of your most difficult challenges—those you feel you can't achieve. Pray through each one, asking God to provide the resources He has promised. Now with that greater faith, expect the Lord to help meet the need as you obey Him to a greater degree.

CHAPTER 7

UNDERSTANDING OUR MARCHING ORDERS

1. We serve Christ for many reasons, all based on what He has done for us and who He is. List ten reasons why you want to give your all for Jesus Christ—five of them should relate to His character and attributes and five should describe what He has done for you (both in the Scriptures and personally).

2. What are the main fears and excuses you have regarding your inability to share the gospel as much as you should? How do many Christian activities tend to minimize the burden or need to evangelize others? How can you connect or integrate your fellowship and spiritual disciplines with reaching the lost?

3. Jesus Christ and His character is central to your Christian life. How do you consciously attempt to show forth the person of Christ in your everyday life? Would an unbeliever know you were a Christian or know what Christ is like based upon your behavior, as well as your words? What do the people you work with, or frequently come in contact with, think about the Christ you represent? What do they say about the Christ they see in you?

4. The church is built upon our confession of Christ as the Son of God. How do you function within your church to make the beauty and glory of Christ shine forth? List ways in which your church can grow up together into the full stature of Christ. Since we are His body, how can you as an individual better minister to others in order to grow in Him and help others to do so as well?

5. Based on the five features defining a movement, would you characterize your local church as a movement or an organization? Are you entering into, or currently in the midst of revival? Have you reached the dangerous stage of monument making? What personal steps can you take to aid revival?

CHAPTER 8
THE MISSION AND THE COMMAND

1. We are not called to merely make believers, but to produce full-fledged disciples. Do you often think only about people being saved? Discipleship means the optimum use of gifts, reaching our full potential in being conformed to the image of Christ. How can you bring an individual not only to saving faith in Christ but to full commitment as a follower?

2. The Great Commission can be fulfilled wherever God has put us. In what areas might you be limiting God's power or activity? Do you feel uncomfortable or "fanatical" about sharing even the basic gospel in certain situations? Do you see evangelism as relegated to church or the job of the preacher? Ask God to realign your thinking in these areas. Ask Him to touch your heart with the needs of those around you and to give you the boldness you need.

3. The Great Commission is also universal. Ask God to help you learn more about and pray for different countries, ethnic groups, races, and even religions. See yourself as part of the global army spreading God's kingdom to the far corners of the earth. Pray for reconciliation on a personal level with those who differ from you racially, ethnically, etc.

4. Compassion is so important for the believer. If you have been saved from destruction, how do you feel about your fellow human beings who don't know God? Many have empathy and concern for the temporary needs of this life. What about the eternal destiny of souls? Make a list of people you have

failed in one of the following areas—ignorance, judgment, lack of concern. Seek a new heart.

5. Many people are hungry to discuss spiritual things, especially the person of Jesus Christ. Write out a two-page response to someone who asks why you think Christ is the only answer to the world's needs. Follow the guidelines of the author by making it loving and tender, yet clear and firm. Use this as a guide when you face your next opportunity to witness.

CHAPTER 9

THE POWER SOURCE

1. If the Holy Spirit were removed from your Christian activity, would there be much of a difference? Where are you using your best efforts on God's behalf—but without prayer or yielding to the Spirit's leading? Take two extreme situations—one in which the Holy Spirit was in control and one where you were on your own. What were the chief differences?

2. Do a Bible study on the person and work of the Holy Spirit. Even if you have done this at some time in the past, ask the Holy Spirit to reveal new things about Himself. Write on a piece of paper every new insight you have received, especially as it can be applied to your relationship with the Holy Spirit. Seek His assistance to grow in fellowship.

3. Most Christians want to know the deep truths of God in order to live them and communicate them through their lives. Yet our nature is to do it our way. As you grow in your love relationship with the Holy Spirit (question two) yield to Him and ask specifically that He reveal His truth to you. Analyze the qualitative differences in your study of God's Word.

4. We need to wait for the power from on high. When does pragmatism or even zeal for service cause us to presume that we have the power and should move on? How often have you felt that God is measuring you by productivity and performance, rather than yieldedness and obedience? Think of an instance where you've witnessed but should have waited. Seek God for the right timing.

5. Many of us are not willing to put the time into long-term prayer for God to prepare the hearts of the unsaved. The greatest effectiveness is in our prayers and God's preparation, rather than in our own words. Make a commitment to pray for those for whom you have great concern. Be willing to pray for years, if necessary, for God to change their hearts. What opportunities have you had lately to share the gospel with others? Did you use your opportunity?

CHAPTER 10

UNDER HIS CONTROL

1. Review the list of questions related to "spiritual tiredness" at the beginning of the chapter. Rate yourself from one to ten (ten means the most serious problem) and then summarize how spiritually dry you may be at present. Ask the Holy Spirit to enter every one of these areas to quicken you with His power. Read Romans 8 and Galatians 5.

2. What kind of host are you to the Holy Spirit? He will not force His way into areas of your life. In what rooms of your heart, however small, is He made to feel off-limits? Perhaps you miss His presence by forgetfulness or immaturity. Make a commitment now to seek out any and every area of your words, thoughts, or actions that may be off-limits and invite His control of them.

3. Being filled with the Holy Spirit is the key to a complete character transformation into the image of Christ. Which character qualities mentioned as elements of the fruit of the Spirit are you lacking to various degrees? Ask God's Spirit to fill you in all circumstances so that all the fruit (character qualities) will appear in increasing measure.

4. Having the Spirit dwell within us and being filled continually are two different matters. Though He has a permanent place, we need to be filled continuously to live the Christian life. Ask the Holy Spirit to remind you to pray to be regularly empowered so you will have strength to do God's will at all times.

5. You may need at this moment to be filled afresh with God's Spirit to grow in character or to complete some task for Him. The key obstacle to His outpoured visitation is your sin. He can't fill an impure vessel. Ask Him to bring to mind your sins so you may confess, repent, and be cleansed through faith in Christ.

CHAPTER 11

THE PATH
TO SIGNIFICANCE

1. Have you ever tried to determine the significance of your life? Has your opinion of what makes it significant changed through the years? Have you found that your concept of the significance of your life changes based on your level of obedience to God's leading? How? What can you learn from that?

2. The quest for significance, even for the sake of Christ, can be very dangerous to our Christian growth. Besides competition and dominance, name some other sins or distractions where false measurement may hurt us. Why are loyalty and faithfulness more important?

3. We tend to look at what we own, how we're recognized, who we're connected with, or what we do, to achieve identity. Remind yourself that you own nothing and you are only a steward for God. In this light, analyze how trustworthy you are with managing His possessions.

4. When you evaluate your life's performance, begin by the author's three principles: no human court, no self-judgment, God alone is the judge. Ask God's revelation through His Spirit as to how you measure up in the critical areas—servanthood, stewardship, and trustworthiness. Where He reveals a lack, ask for His grace and His forgiveness.

5. Ultimately, our significance does not depend on what we decide to do for God. He has a plan and will test our compliance and willingness to serve Him. Why are your accomplish-

ments an invalid measure of your significance? Why may some people who look insignificant or appear to be failures be prominent in the kingdom of heaven? Does your success focus on tangible results or the approval of others? Ask God to make Himself your sole source of approval.

CHAPTER 12
A PLEA FOR PERSPECTIVE

1. No matter what hard times you may endure, or where you may fail, God has a unique plan for your life and wants to use you in a significant way. In what unique ways has God given you opportunities to respond and contribute to His kingdom?

2. You have one brief chance on this earth to make a difference. The first part of your strategy should be a plan to know God's eternal Word. The second part is to become strongly aware of the times in which you live. Then apply the first to the second. Start by practice—take an event or trend in society and seek God to bring it under the judgment and scrutiny of His Word.

3. Hardship and suffering should also be considered in God's purposes. Endurance proves our character. Rather than seeking to avoid the inevitable, ask God for the strength to make the most of it by His grace in a way that is pleasing to Him. Study the purposes of suffering found throughout the Scriptures.

4. The meaning of the Cross, both as a key part of the gospel message and as part of our lives, is neglected and is also a deep mystery. Find a good book or article on the Cross. Then do a study historically and theologically for greater background. Ask God to use the Cross to bring you closer to Him and His Son, Jesus Christ.

5. Finally, remember the purpose of life. True fulfillment comes in consistently doing His will. As Paul finished the course faithfully, we too should pray for faithfulness and obedience. Write down a new insight or meaning for both of these terms—faithfulness and obedience—in your life.

Moody Press, a ministry of Moody Bible Institute,
is designed for education, evangelization, and edification.
If we may assist you in knowing more about Christ
and the Christian life, please write us without obligation:
Moody Press, c/o MLM, Chicago, Illinois 60610.